Just Manage It!
The 'YOU' Factor

If You Cannot Manage
Yourself
You Cannot Manage Others

Colm McCormack

Preface

All around the world - whether in London, New York, Dublin, wherever – lots of people are making the same mistakes. And these mistakes cost every single one of us extortionate amounts. Conventional wisdom has become popular nonsense. Low-cost, quick-fix, speed - and many other misapplied mindsets - are pulling us all down. But we're so pleased with ourselves and our achievements that we've not only ignored our deficiencies: we have totally lost any ability to recognize them. We cannot see just how far we have strayed onto the wrong course.

Our attention and focus have been hijacked by those chanting *leader, leader, leader*. We have been blinded by our new found idolatry and have forsaken all common sense for an opportunity to dance around the new golden calf. We believe ourselves to have become so sophisticated that simple basic principles are now beneath us. We no longer see any need to install foundations: just run the damn thing, get it done, and massacre them on costs to grow our margins. Keep the share price up, hire people just like us and work longer and harder than everyone else.

The roots are to be found in the Business Schools: let all management books start with the history of management – the Taylors, the Fayols, the Hawthorne studies - but for God sake don't start at the real beginning: the person himself – the manager! Teach them about perfect competition. Tell them to set price where marginal revenue equals marginal cost.[1] Get them to specialize in functions.[2] Tell them strategy can only be implemented through people but don't teach them how to interact or communicate with people. Tell them the *Art of War* by Sun Tzu is all they really need. Then divert and make them feel good with nonsense about work-life balance and other such misinterpreted and wrongly placed ideals. Keep dumping clones out of the Business Schools into the world. It doesn't matter if they're sociopathic, sadistic, mentally or emotionally unbalanced - unfit in so many ways. Just keep teaching them the same crap, let *them* tell *us* what they need, pull in as much money for the school as possible and to hell with the consequences!

---

[1] For an interesting discussion on these economic points see: Ormerod, P. (2005).
[2] By Functions I mean the functions of organizations and the subjects as taught in business schools, i.e. strategy, Human Resources, Finance, etc. Such functions can be *administered* from a back room without much or any interaction with other human beings.

Contents

Introduction – Living *Is* Managing..7

Chapter 1   Get a Life!...22

Chapter 2   Constantly Reassess - Toward Creating the
Psychological Default Setting............................51

Chapter 3   *All* Blame Migrates 71

Chapter 4   Positive Consistency..80

Chapter 5   The Three Muddy Puddles 93

Chapter 6   Communication 105

Chapter 7   Context Sensitive - Toward Creating
"Context Intelligent" Managers.......................130

Chapter 8   Questions to Ask Yourself 147

Chapter 9   *Every*body Sets an Example 171

Chapter 10   Leader, Leader, Leader –
Chanting the Wrong Mantra? 190

Conclusion 205
Bibliography..221

Introduction
Living *Is* Managing

Once Upon a Time…

When I was about ten years old, I watched two of my uncles installing patio doors at the back of our house. But the doors just would not work properly. It turned out that one side of the door frame sat against a brick wall that had been constructed during previous renovations. The first line of blocks was not level thereby leading to the wall bending slightly to one side as it rose. You couldn't see this with the naked eye. The answer seemed simple: level the door frame and then fill in any gap between the frame and the wall. Instead, my uncles took out the frame, tore down the wall, and started again from scratch. None of us could understand why they would put themselves through so much trouble. Their argument, however, was that the obvious solution was nothing but a quick-fix band-aid type remedy; the crooked foundation blocks would simply lead to a lifetime of crisis fixing. They had the wall down and rebuilt in less than half a day. They probably would have spent more time constantly adjusting the filling between the frame and the wall and constantly re-checking that everything was level and in-line.

What we see from this little story is a willingness to go back to the simple basic principles of building: a bad foundation will cause a lifetime of heartache. It didn't take long to assess the situation, to discover the problem, to make the right decision and then do what was required to ensure a pain-free future. In your daily life and when running a business, however, the thoughts of having to look at your own behavior, the way you make decisions, the way you react to people around you, are similar to the thoughts of coming near the end of a renovation job and facing the prospects of pulling it down and starting again. Most of us simply carry on. We choose to spend more time quick-fixing and band-aiding the problem than we would have spent getting to the root cause. Put the fire out and move to the next one: that's the workplace mentality. It's also a pretty good reflection of our family lives. So long as that next problem is different than the one we just band-aided, we never attract the blame.

The World Outside Our Windows

50% or more of the western world are working in the wrong jobs.[3] We in the West are experiencing unprecedented levels of wealth, yet the greatest percentage in history of people who feel lost – that their lives are pointless and have no meaning – exists right here, right now, today. Research tells us that people in their 30s and 40s are unhappy with life to the extent they are more unhappy than teenagers and old age pensioners. Despite buying power having almost tripled since the 1950s, the average American's sense of happiness has remained almost unchanged.[4] The World Health

---

[3] The Conference Board, in 2007, revealed that only 50% of American workers were satisfied with their jobs. – See: http://www.huffingtonpost.com/2007/09/24/what-to-do-when-you-hate-_n_65649.html In the same year, Americans were said to "…hate their jobs more than ever before…"See: http://www.livescience.com/health/070226_hate_jobs.html
[4] See Myers (2008) p. 428.

Organization estimates depression will be the biggest disability in North America by 2020.[5] A frighteningly high percentage of us are constantly dehydrated without knowing it: we start the day with coffee – a diuretic – then continue quenching the resulting thirst throughout the day with sugared soft drinks or more coffee. More and more rich kids in the western world are heading for the psychiatrists or analysts chair. Mental and eating disorders are becoming the new teenage pastime.

The approach – or lack thereof –people take toward their own lives really is quite baffling. We research vacations. We even read brochures, test drive cars, and chat with other car owners. But when it comes to life we go, at best, for wishy-washy vagueness or, at worst, we just go with the flow. Business schools will tell you the ideal business situation is one in which the personal goals of the employees are in line with or complementary to the goals of the organization. But if 50% or more of us are in the wrong jobs, just what does reality on the ground really look like? If people are dehydrated, overfed and under nourished – and many other things suggesting they can't manage their own lives – should they be allowed manage other people?

How Do You Know Whether You Can Manage Yourself or Not?

People who cannot properly manage themselves waste countless hours dealing with the fallout of their own behavior. Studies comparing effective managers with those who derail reveal interesting findings we should keep in mind:[6]

---

[5] http://www.who.int/mental_health/management/depression/definition/en/
[6] See Yukl (2006) Chapt. 7, 187-188, referring to McCall & Lombardo (1983), Lombardo & McCauley (1988) and Van Velsor & Leslie (1995). Table constructed here for presentation purposes and ease of use.

Emotional Stability	Those who derailed were more prone to emotional outbursts, inconsistent behavior and handled stress poorly.
Defensiveness	Admitting mistakes and learning from them were not high on the agendas of managers who derailed; cover-ups and blame were more in their line.
Interpersonal Skills	Managers who derailed were less tactful, less considerate, and less sensitive toward others.

How many managers do we know who fly off the handle, don't admit to mistakes, blame everyone around them, and more? To these three simple findings we can now add things such as anger, addiction, external locus of control, a regular ignorance of context, regularly setting unsuitable examples, an inability to manage their own personal finances, an unwillingness to see themselves as possibly being part of any problem or as needing to improve and change. The list, of course, is not limited but those ten or so points are of crucial importance. Most of these are *not* things they teach you in Business or Management School. It is for these reasons we will look at topics and models such as:

- Correcting the Human Default Life Plan;
- The Five Constituency Model for Observation in the Workplace;
- Creating Context Intelligent Managers;
- The Ten-Ps of Constituency and Context Awareness;
- Context Ignorance and the Steps toward Ineffective Results;
- Positive and Negative Consistency;
- The Power of Positive Social Contagion;
- Listening Fitness;
- The Co-Activity Syndrome;
- The Dangerous Power of Perceptions;
- The Importance of Organizational Politics, Ego, and Confrontation;

➢ Warping the Psychological Contract.

We will dip into business, management, psychology, philosophy, and more. We will take pieces from everywhere, take a rounded approach, dismiss some of what we already *know*, and go further. As Friedrich Nietzsche indicates:

> The philosopher believes that the value of his philosophy lies in the whole, in the building: posterity discovers it in the bricks with which he built and which are then often used again for better building:…that is to say, that that building can be destroyed and nonetheless possess value as material.[7]

With Nietzsche's words ringing in our ears, we can say that the failure rates in managing people can be reduced via a four-point system modelled on Risk Homeostasis theory[8] reworded to suit our present discussion:[9]

➢ Increase the perceived benefits of effective management by teaching and demonstrating its benefits;
➢ Decrease the perceived hassle, effort, cost and reduced speed of moving toward effective management;
➢ Increase the perceived hassle, effort, cost and reduced speed of the current ineffective managerial practices;
➢ Decrease all perceived benefits of the current ineffective managerial practices.

---

[7] Thompson (1995).
[8] See Wilde, G. (2001). *Target Risk 2: A New Psychology of Health and Safety: What Works, What Doesn't and Why*…Toronto: PDE Publications. Sourced from: Carr (2004).
[9] I have been careful throughout this book not to suggest that emotional intelligence is the sum total solution for effective management despite many of the items listed under the emotional competence inventory appearing at one time or another (See: Goleman, 2004). Emotional intelligence is but a part of the required overall mix.

All four points, and everything appearing within this book, relate to both home and work reflecting our philosophy that living *is* managing. It makes no sense to emerge from chaos in the morning, go to work to manage, and then return home to chaos in the evening. Management principles work everywhere. The roadmap we will follow is this:

- Learn the most common mistakes people make;
- Reflect to see how we too make those mistakes;
- Observe others over time in order to bring about self-regulation and reinforcement and to spot these mistakes in others;
- Finally, start influencing others in a positive way from a safe and secure personal base via suitable example setting, suitable and effective management and teaching.

And it is an effective roadmap. Analysis of faulty thinking and practicing new behaviors can bring about positive change.

Your Personal Leadership and Management Brand

In essessence, your personal brand is what people say about you when you are not in the room; it is the everytime guaranteed experience of you – your style, your approach. As with any other brand, people need to know what differentiates you from the pack; they need a clear sense of who you serve; a clear sense of your guaranteed minimum standards and a sense of the consistent value you offer the organization through this specific, personalized brand.

This first book sets the foundation for this particular topic; a topic built upon further in book two: the PEOPLE factor.[10] It is

---

[10] Just Manage It! The 'PEOPLE' Factor: *Leading and Managing the People Around You*: McCormack, 2010.

essential that you take time getting this topic right; install the foundation now so that moving later lead and manage the people around you will see you handle such an endeavour in the most suitable and effective way possible; when people encounter you, you will already be a more rounded and developed individual.

What You *Should* be Managing

Let us now consider a diagram I have constructed – the Hidden Self diagram - that will aid us in this chapter and throughout the book:[11]

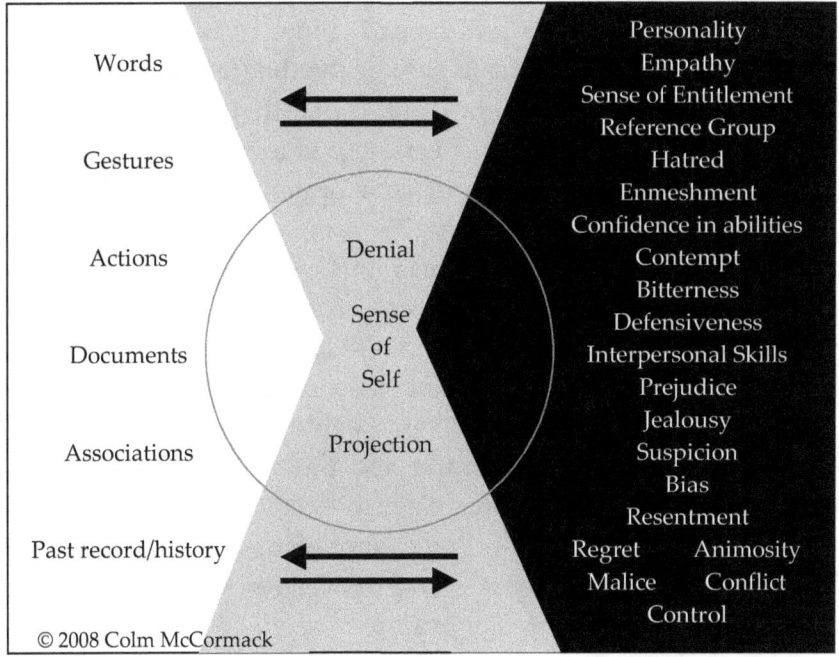

When we see a person behaving in a particular way, saying various things, producing work results, the part we see is actually

---

[11] The list of items contained within the diagram is not intended to be an exhaustive one.

quite small. What lies in the shadows, however, can be far more important by multiples. Look at the words on the left side of the diagram – the words that are out in the light. If you read the diagram from left to right, through the center and into the dark, things become very interesting indeed. Everything we see a person do, hear them say, or watch them produce, must first run through the filter at the center of the diagram – Denial, Sense of Self, and Projection. The strength and effect of this filter is determined by everything in the shadows: the words on the right-hand side of the diagram. We can also read from right to left: all of these things hidden within a person produce a filter of particular strength and effect that determines their overt actions, words, results.

Most managers will spend time focusing on managing everything on the left-hand side of the diagram when in truth it is everything on the right-hand side that carries far greater importance. You get to uncover these hidden aspects by interacting with the humans working in your organization, by observing, by engaging in effective listening[12] – things you will start to become very familiar with as you read this book. More importantly, all those labels on the right-hand side of the diagram apply to you and if you cannot manage yourself, these labels become warning badges to alert others. The right-hand side of the Hidden Self diagram contains the items that motivate people to engage in the behavior you will have to manage. But you must discover these things in yourself first. We will move later to look at them in others in book two: The PEOPLE Factor. You cannot manage yourself effectively if you are unaware of what lies in the shadows governing your own behavior and attitudes. For example, are you too defensive? Do you argue and obstruct people even when they are trying to help make one of your suggestions better? Or do you have trouble trusting

---

[12] We will look at Effective Listening later in Chapter 6 on Communication, and then again in The 'PEOPLE' Factor – book two in this *Just Manage It!* series.

people without any prior history of these particular people having let you down? Moving to the center of the diagram we can conclude that if you are in Denial over such examples and issues, then your Sense of Self may not be quite what it should and you may very well Project unnecessary things onto those around you by way of what you do, say and produce.

But Why "Management"?

After years in business why on earth would any manager want to hear about simple basics, about their own behavior, about their ego, about the need to constantly reassess, about any of those things? It is one of the most tragic ironies of the business world that everyone in it is too busy to stop and make their lives easier and less busy. Sounds funny doesn't it? *"Sorry, I'm too busy to make myself less busy"*, or, *"Sorry, I'm too busy digging a hole to stop digging and step out of it"*.

And there are more managers out there than there are people who know how to manage. That's the reality. And it's a worrying one. "Manager" has been stretched to cover too many people: people incapable of managing. But that's only part of the story. Generally, the Business and Management Schools aren't teaching people how to manage anyway so what's out there is not so much management versus non-management material: it's all just different levels of unsuitability. [13]

I believe in one particular rule: if you can't manage yourself you can't manage others. Think about this for a moment. How many people do you and I know in our own lives who cannot even confront their own parents?[14] How many times have you and I,

---

[13] Most of us are incredibly busy and incredibly short on time but not incredibly successful at what we do.
[14] This can become a particular problem in family businesses when a parent lingers after retirement. Often, their continued presence is a malignant one destroying confidence and

dear reader, been that person? And that being the case, why should you or I – or those other people we know – be allowed out to manage others? The only way such people manage is by stomping around the playground frightening all the other children when they don't get their way. Or they'll simply hide away from everyone, playing the ostrich game, avoiding confrontation, and letting the whole place go to hell.

We're all familiar with the idea that we keep moving through bad times until we come out the other side.[15] But this has been incorrectly applied for many years now. Keep going does not mean keep going in the same direction doing the same thing. But that's precisely what far too many people do, both in life and at work. Being declared a parent, a teacher, or a manager, does not declare you to be sound, mature, or well balanced; but that is precisely what so many of us automatically assume.

The very act of living *is* managing. From hearing the morning alarm, to showering, getting dressed, going to work, eating breakfast - they are all accomplished through the act of management. If there is a power outage or we encounter road works on the way to the office, we manage it. But this ability seems to get lost somewhere amongst all the other things that afflict us throughout the day. Why is that? Why do we manage some things but then stand like deer in the headlights for everything else?

Stretching Mintzberg: the *Real* Starting Point

When I was lecturing, I would ask students to raise their hands if they had ever suffered at the hands of a bad manager. Most had. Then I asked whether any of them had suffered because of a bad teacher. Again, quite a few hands went up. Then I asked

---

undermining whatever little authority actually exists. They also enable others to go around the new "boss" thereby creating further problems.

[15] The concept of keep pushing on through hell is attributed to Winston Churchill.

the rhetorical question: who has suffered at the hands of a bad parent? Now imagine teaching management to someone who has suffered all three: bad parents, bad teachers, and bad managers.

It is woefully inadequate to dive straight into management topics without considering the people we are teaching. What if – in an extreme case - a person is sadistic, unbalanced, unhinged? It doesn't seem to matter – teach them anyway. They arrive inadequate, we teach them, and then we complain about their later behavior.[16]

Business schools don't have filters to detect such people. We have the GMAT and other such partially adequate nonsense. Mintzberg, in his superb book *Managers Not MBAs*, is on the right track but, for me, is in danger of starting too late in the chain.[17] Teaching and developing management skills on the grounds that people must have had "experience" managing is dangerous. It misses the point entirely. Some want to manage out of ego, a desire for power, a desire to become wealthy. Some because they're sick of being walked on, because they have something to prove, because they want to become the success their parent, or that teacher, or that idiot manager said they could never become. All questionable. All undetectable to the business school system.[18]

If I am an asshole – fine. But if I have children, then *they* suffer. If I am a football coach, then *more* suffer. But if I'm a manager, the extent of my corrupting influence starts to expand alarmingly – whether such negative influence is intended or unwitting. But our

---

[16] To paraphrase: foolish are they who build on sand.
[17] Mintzberg really has written a fantastic book. I could only find myself disagreeing with him on fewer points than a man has fingers on one hand. Revolution is notorious for devouring her own children and advocates of change who stay too long within the system start to become viewed as part of the system. Nonetheless: penitenze agite!
[18] We must also be mindful of differing definitions of *effective* managers and *successful* managers. In choosing managers on the grounds of experience managing, we must be careful as to our decisions surrounding experienced effective managers or experienced successful managers.

quick-fire society misses this crucial point. At Trinity College in Ireland, counseling psychology students must undergo ongoing personal counseling as part of their training.[19] It ensures they don't project any personal nonsense onto the people they will end up "helping". But not teachers, not those who run kindergartens, not priests, not managers: people with more influence than the average person are allowed exert control over the lives of others without first ever having to account for their own fitness to do so. Fitness to manage is simply declared by experience and an academic qualification of one form or another. And the proof was to be seen every semester when I asked my three-pronged parents-teacher-manager question. The majority of hands *always* went up. And we suffer under a lot of such people because they themselves have suffered. They project their suffering onto us. And so the cycle continues.

And this will be our starting point: you should not be allowed to manage others if you cannot manage yourself. We will put quality control to the front of the process. We will touch on items such as locus of control, blame, taking responsibility, planning our personal lives, dangerous words and phrases, and moving away from negativity. Dealing with these issues will enable us sidestep the pitfalls that cause managers to derail. Dealing with these issues will enable you to manage yourself effectively thereby giving you the ability to manage others effectively.

---

[19] There are of course many other colleges running similar such programs but I do have particular knowledge of the Trinity set-up in this regard.

Stretching Stewart and her Theory of Demands, Constraints, Choices[20]

Generally, demands are defined in terms of job characteristics and the things the manager must do to stay in the job.[21] Throughout this book, I want to make it clear that when referring to the demands made of managers I am also encompassing irrational demands made by emotionally charged workers ignorant or uncaring of the fact that a lot of what they are complaining about has nothing to do with their manager or the workplace. For example, as a manager you will often be confronted by a worker seeking a pay raise because he has recently taken out a mortgage to buy a new house. This of course was *his* choice and nothing to do with you. But the demands made of you as a result – dealing with an angry, frustrated, disillusioned employee who is now souring the atmosphere on a daily basis – should not be dismissed simply because what he is complaining about has nothing to do with the workplace. The fact that you will often be the target for blame in so many non-work related matters that make little sense is irrelevant: demands made of you in your managerial role will, for the purposes of this book, extend to demands of any nature – role and duty related, emotion based, and the downright daft.

Are Medical Schools Taking a Giant Leap for Mankind?

Medical schools have started to take an interesting approach. In Ireland, for example, the top universities have started to question whether the brightest students actually make the best doctors.

---

[20] See the extensive work and numerous books of Professor Rosemary Stewart of Templeton College, University of Oxford in the United Kingdom. A brief overview can be had from: *Demands, Constraints, Choices and Discretion: An Introduction to the Work of Rosemary Stewart.* The Leadership Quarterly, 14, (2003) 193-238.

[21] As defined by Steward herself in: An Introduction to the Work of Rosemary Stewart. Pg. 200.

Focus has now turned toward their "bedside manner" or, for the purposes of our discussion here, toward whether students can manage themselves effectively to ensure they can deal with patients effectively. Prospective medical students must now sit the three module, two and a half hour long HPAT (Health Professions Admission Test) within two years preceding admission onto their courses.[22]

While this is a very encouraging development, there is of course the danger it will take the same route as IQ, GMAT, and other such tests, i.e. decrease in practical relevance and simply become money spinners. But the content of the test, particularly the module on Interpersonal Reasoning, is to be commended in spirit at least.[23]

Some Final Thoughts

A lot of what we will cover here is not touched upon by the business schools. But the point should be clear by now: start at the beginning and make sure that a person can manage themselves before allowing them to manage others.[24]

Whether you've never studied management but are running your own company or have business credentials up the yin-yang and want to get up-to-date, this book is for you. This is a management book for the real person living in the real world. It starts where all books ought to start: at the beginning. The first chapter is entitled *Get a Life*. The beginning must be the person him

---

[22] Test administered by ACER (Australian Council for Educational Research). For a brochure on this test, see: http://www.hpat-ireland.acer.edu.au/images/documents/hpat_brochure.pdf

[23] A brief indication as to the type of questions asked can be gleaned from: http://www.hpat-ireland.acer.edu.au/index.php?option=com_content&view=category&layout=blog&id=5&Itemid=4

[24] It is not too far a stretch of the imagination to operate under the hypothesis that a lot of today's social problems can find their roots in poorly structured work, dysfunctional and harmful organizational culture, and bad management.

or herself – the person who wants to be a manager or have authority over others. If their life is a mess due to their own thinking and behavior, then why let them control anything else? Many books skip this part. They start somewhere in the middle ignoring the fact that the person they're trying to help is not being helped.

The book will then move toward creating a psychological default setting in the manager that enables him/her to reassess constantly with little effort. It will move onto the concept that all blame migrates, that consistency of approach can be classified as either positive or negative, and culminate with the idea that when the manager has gained the ability to manage himself properly, he may then turn toward managing others via suitable example setting, positive social contagion, and more.

Managing is about adding value. The trick is not to expect people to be extraordinary: it's getting everyday people to perform in an extraordinary way - there's a world of difference!

Chapter 1
Get A Life!

"When it comes to character issues, work on your weaknesses. When it comes to talents, go with your strengths."[25]

Not managing your own life will see you distracted, under unnecessary stress and pressure, and unhappy and unfulfilled on numerous fronts. All of this dissatisfaction can then be projected onto others thereby making you an unsuitable manager. Managing yourself allows you to avoid all the pitfalls that cause other managers to derail and enables you move toward a greater ability to lead and manage others more effectively.

Taking Hold of the Reins

If you are going to manage then you need to *believe* you can manage. That's where your locus of control comes in. And you're going to have to develop the ability to determine the type of locus in people around you if you are to lead and manage them effectively.

An *external* locus of control in a person suggests they believe that what happens to them in life is due to factors external to them as a person. In other words, fate, other people, the system. And we know lots of these people. *"He makes me feel so angry"*, *"I feel great today because the phones hardly rang all day"* – these are the phrases

---

[25] Maxwell (2004) p. 10.

spoken by people with external locus of control. Note how they themselves are not viewed as the source of their own emotions.[26] Take a look at this very interesting example:

> ...we do not answer a phone because it rings; we answer it because we want to...The ring does have a purpose, but it is not to make you answer. It is to give you information, to tell you that someone out there wants to talk to someone here...But information is not control...Since information does not make us do anything, we can choose to ignore it or act on it any way we see fit.[27]

An *internal* locus of control, however, suggests a person believes that their life is influenced more by factors internal to themselves. Their emotions do not just *happen* to them. Even in a volatile industry where things change by the hour, such people still hold onto the belief that they can control how they perceive and react to things – control still rests with them no matter what turns up. And this is important. Watch the look on business students faces when you tell them there is only one thing on the planet they can ever fully control.[28]

Someone with a strong internal locus of control might be heard to say, "*I make my own luck*". Such a person will reword the sentences spoken by the externally controlled person so that: "He makes me feel so angry" might become, "He behaves like a real jerk but I control my own moods", and "I feel great today because the

---

[26] It is my view Psychologists and the like must be incredibly careful to ask "How did you feel?" and *not* "How did *that* make you feel?" – there are occasions when the second might promote an external locus of control and put the "happening" of emotions into the hands of events, people, and things external to the person seeking help.

[27] Glasser (1998) p. 17. An interesting example given that today people seem unable to ignore text messages on their cell phones or fret endlessly if they realize they don't have the phone with them. It seems so many people allow their phones to control *them* rather than the other way around.

[28] Yourself – your emotions, your perceptions, your reactions, etc. Tough to take considering so many definitions of management contain the word "controlling". Note, however, I have not mentioned "influence" here, only "control".

phones hardly rang all day" might become, "I don't care how busy the phones are. <u>If I want to feel great I'll feel great</u>".

Giving people or things – anything external to your person – control over how you feel is daft, a waste of time and energy, and setting yourself up to be the constant victim. It allows you to blame, to become defensive and encourages anger, disillusionment and a variety of other emotional instabilities; the very things that, as we saw in the introduction, can cause a manager to derail. This is not how you manage yourself and certainly not how you become an effective manager.[29] Let me give you an example.

Jon is an assistant manager. He took the great step of going back to school at night to earn his degree. But this achievement seems to make little difference to his employer. In Jon's eyes, he is being treated very unfairly and is wasting his talents by not using his new found knowledge. This is the fault of the company he works for and his senior managers. They are to blame. They are holding him back. Several years later, Jon still works for the same company, in the same managerial position, doing the same job. Except now he suffers from severe migraines. The doctors can't find any cause. He's been for scans, blood tests, changed his diet, has taken time off work to relax. But the truth may very well be that deep inside Jon is unhappy. Will he admit that he allows his job, and being undervalued in it, to dictate his emotions? There are other things he really wants to do. He has spoken to me about them many times. But he feels locked-in due to commitments, expectations, fear of disappointing others. If he had an internal locus of control he would not be feeling the way he is. And he certainly would not be suffering debilitating, and medically

---

[29] But there must also be a limit on personal control. Many people may already feel that they have more control than is warranted by reality, and they may be subject in the future to strong trauma when they discover that they cannot control such things as corporate failures, diseases, etc. - Rotter, J. B. *Generalized expectancies for internal versus external control of reinforcement.* Psychological Monographs, 1966

unexplainable, headaches. His entire life seems to be in the hands of other people. His emotions are controlled by everything external to him – his bosses, the organization, his family. He is blaming others for his situation and suffering as a result. Do you think Jon should be allowed manage others? Or are you inclined to overlook his attitude simply because he has years of experience in a managerial position?

Our Aimless Default-Plan

Wandering aimlessly through life creates so many problems. Again my reference to emerging from chaos, managing at work, and then returning home to chaos. We know that ship wrecked survivors in a life raft will survive longer if they set themselves daily tasks, duties, set routines. Those who sit idly by awaiting rescue have been shown to have a smaller chance of survival. When you don't have any goals you can have poor sense of direction.[30]

As humans, our default plan for life often seems to be this, or something very like it: Born, Go to school, Get a job, Get married, Have kids, Retire, See what happens.

No wonder half of us are in the wrong jobs and managing the wrong things. No wonder retirement finds so many of us with spouses we don't know anymore, kids we don't recognize, bad pensions, poor health. It's the *see what happens* aspect that causes so much damage. And it doesn't just appear at the end of the list. Instead, it can permeate it entirely.[31] See the following diagram:

---

[30] Death anxiety is inversely proportional to life satisfaction (Scaturo) 2005 quoting: Yalom, 1980, p.207.

[31] A student once asked me, "But how do I know if I'm in the wrong job?" The answer seemed easy – if it's crap and you hate it. But the flippancy of the answer betrays the genius of the question. Sometimes the right job feels wrong because other factors in our lives are not what they should be. Just as unhappiness in the workplace can (incorrectly) manifest itself as a complaint about money (whether the complainer realizes this or not) so too can

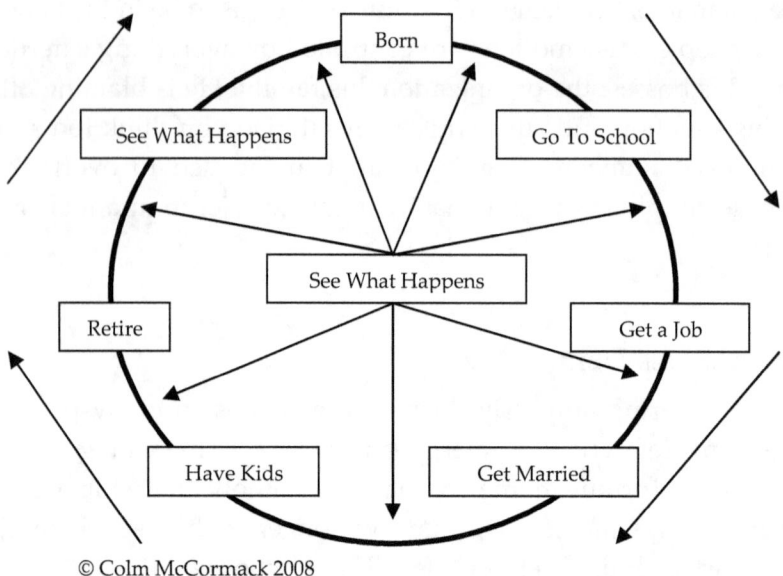

© Colm McCormack 2008

Start With YOU

Let us go back to me asking my three-pronged teacher-manager-parent question. After asking it, I would write the date on the left side of the whiteboard. I would get the students (I mostly taught experienced workers and executives) to tell me why they were in the class. The answers always centered on looking for a pay rise, a promotion – all career focused. Then, on the right hand side of the board, I would write "65". I would then tell them to imagine they retired yesterday and today is their first day of freedom. I would get them to describe their life in retirement to me. And the answers were usually the same too: rich, big house, successful, respected, made it to the CEO position, etc.

---

unhappiness in one aspect of our lives manifest itself as a feeling of unhappiness with our job.

I asked, "Who here has a life plan?" It got them to focus on themselves not on some abstract idea or case study. By focusing upon their own lives they instantly have appreciation for the idea of managing themselves before managing others. And it's a great place to start and build from. Shared experiences in the classroom always revealed the same common mistakes and perceptions. If they learn the pitfalls and then plan for their own lives, they will spot disorganization and turmoil in others.

You will have noticed that people usually point to career-centered reasons for coming back to Business School. And they usually point to financial and career outcomes upon reaching retirement. But when I point out to them that they have said nothing about health, about family, about hobbies, etc, there is usually a recognition that these things suffer along the way. When do we decide to look after our health, our family, our own personal time and hobbies? When we get to retirement? But by then any health problems or family issues might have been around for many years. These are all things you have to do in business and management – setting targets, monitoring progress and taking corrective actions. Why do these things at work but not in your own life? If life sucks, then refusing to risk making it better leaves you sitting there without any justifiable reasons to complain.[32]

Already, we have come across many common mistakes made by people. The big one is having no plan or sense of direction. This

---

[32] A student once asked, "But what if I don't know what I want to do in life?" This is becoming an alarmingly common question. There are two dangers for people thinking this way: 1) they pause until the answer presents itself; 2) they put *everything* on hold. Not knowing what they want to do in life automatically becomes an excuse not to plan on any of the other fronts. Just because you can't decide on which career to pursue does not mean you ignore your health, family, self, finances, etc. Just like strategy students who can't decide under which P.E.S.T.E.L. heading a particular factor should go: they leave it to the side until later but more often than not forget about that factor entirely. The key point is just get the factor up onto the board so that it is in your contemplation. A pause in managing your life usually equates, at best, to months, and at worst, to never being considered again.

leads to big problems. First, if life is crap then it needs to change. If your money situation, your health, your family, your personal life, are not quite what they should be then admit that things are not going great. Take responsibility now for making them better. Second, if you are unhappy then over time your family will become unhappy. Third, if you are unhappy then as a manager your subordinates are becoming unhappy too. Fourth, allowing such matters to fester, denying they exist, snapping at people, etc, all see you managing unnecessary things and creating more problems for yourself and for others.

You can't get a good result on many fronts in life if you don't practice goal setting across all aspects of your life. Thinking that little surrenders and no planning are harmless is a dangerous mindset to adopt. All of these things can have a devastating cumulative effect. And this devastation usually presents itself in the guise of a person seeking to lead and manage others.

Seeing the Full Picture

By developing a life plan across numerous fronts (just like cross-functional planning in organizations), you have a unified and inter-linked collection of things to aim for. You have a definite sense of direction. You have something to measure your progress – or lack thereof – against. In other words, you can *manage* your life. You've adopted an internal locus of control. You will avoid anything that does not move you in the right direction. Management skills at work and at home are not mutually exclusive: they should support and reinforce each other. You manage at work, so too should you manage your personal life. Doing so helps you avoid your health suffering because of work, for example, or family problems causing your progress at work to slow or grind to a halt.

In order to demonstrate this idea of work and personal issues requiring management, and to show how it is up to *you* to manage both, I have constructed the following diagram which helps to explain this:

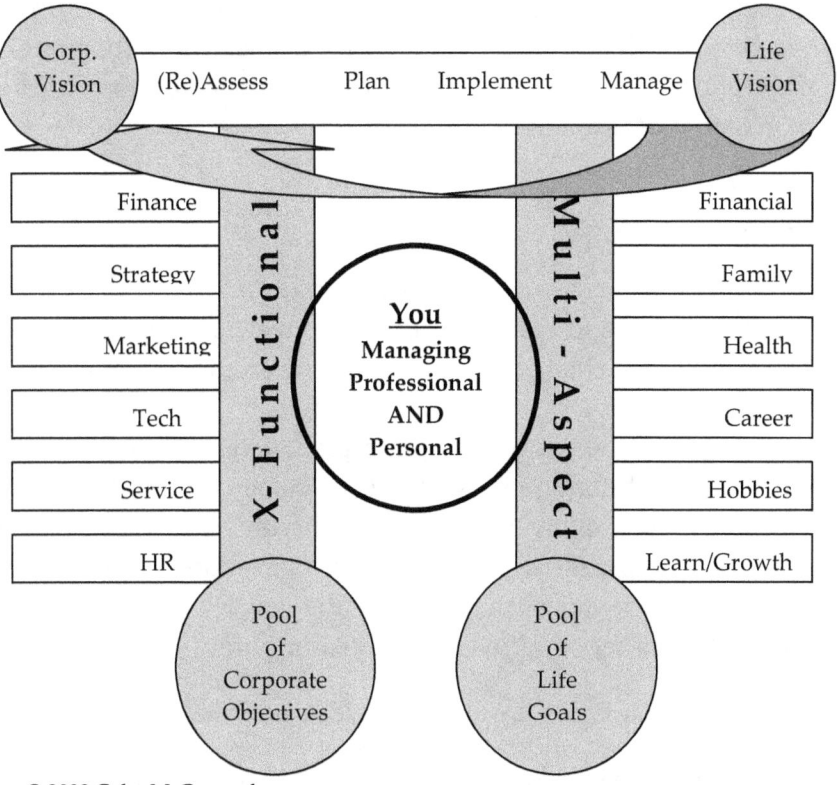

© 2008 Colm McCormack

Starting at the top of the model, an organization has a vision – so too should the person. Planning across the various functions – cross-functional planning – is mirrored in personal life by planning across multiple aspects of life such as health, family, career. This leads to a pool of Life Goals in personal life mirrored by a pool of cross-functional Corporate Objectives. All goals and objectives are constantly subject to reassessment and control. From this model we see how professional and personal life run in parallel at exactly the same time. Therefore, they *must* be managed to obtain the best overall outcome. Be very much aware, however, that it is the right-hand side of the model that gets ignored as work pressures and stresses come to the fore and the large circle in the center shifts to the left as you start to manage work issues only. But it is precisely the right-hand side of the model that can lead to unhappiness, to distraction, to mood swings and ultimately to unsuitable managerial behavior if ignored.

Not *Balance*, **MIX**

I never like using the word *balance*. It conjures up ideas of fifty/fifty splits and perfect equilibrium. Instead, we should use the word *mix*. Mix changes with context whereas context can render balance ineffective.

Think of the many slices in a pie. Success for a lot of people equates to high-flying jobs with lots of money. But individuals who go too far and allow themselves to become identified primarily with their jobs are lining themselves up for misery. Too many of us allow our work and titles to become the majority source of our self-worth. As clinical psychologist Tony Humphreys points out:

> ...if a manager believes that it is success that makes his self worthy of recognition, a defensive addiction to success emerges and work now becomes a significant source of threat to the self. This manager will strive relentlessly to maintain a successful performance, at the cost of neglect of self, marriage, family, employees and colleagues.[33]

The focus on work can lead to neglect of everything else in the life plan mix. The shock to the system when retirement arrives - if unplanned – is devastating, particularly for men, and is becoming a real issue in the western world. So we need to plan for the future to avoid retirement becoming a nightmare. We also need to plan to

---

[33] Humphreys (2006) p. 30. We will conveniently ignore here any Descartesian problems that might see the Self constitute the immaterial controlling the material.

ensure we enjoy life, achieve things we want to achieve, to get away from the pointless and aimless existence, and to break the *born-school-job-married-kids-retire-see what happens* default setting. We must allow ourselves enjoy the moments between events rather than living in limbo - postphoning happiness and satisfaction until some goal or milestone is achieved. Getting it right in our personal lives sets us up well for getting it right in our work lives. Take a look at the following diagram:

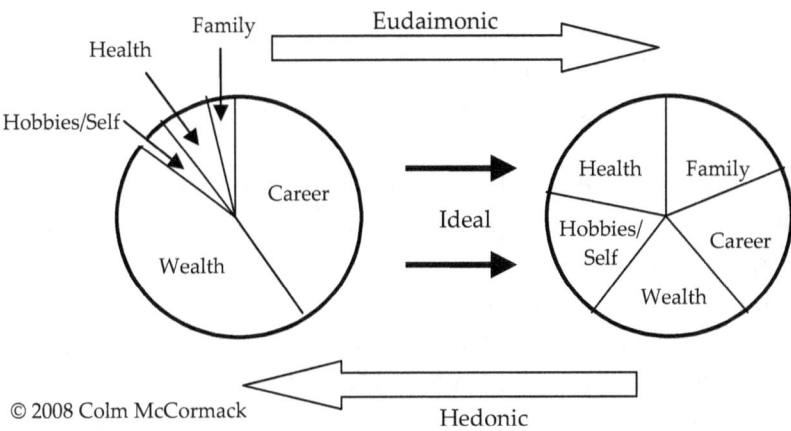

© 2008 Colm McCormack

The circle on the right depicts the ideal. We must be mindful, however, that a person can revert to the circle on the left if tragedy strikes. For example, losing your job will suddenly see career and wealth become top priorities for you. The same with a health scare such as a heart attack or cancer-related illness: suddenly family and health grow in importance with everything else dropping off the radar. But what we are seeing here is a to-ing and fro-ing rather than an overall ideal mix. Too much emphasis on any one factor arises due to poor planning or tragedy/scare: the Hedonic avoidance of pain and seeking of pleasure. At all times, we must aim to move toward the circle on the right: a Eudaimonic-style move toward achieving our full potential on all fronts.[34] Sitting in the circle on the left must only be temporary – months and not years. As a manager, it will soon become your job to move people in that direction too, i.e. if *they* can manage themselves, *your* job becomes easier.

Research[35] shows that the happiest employees are those who work for organizations that supply the following:

- Employee involvement;
- Work life balance – (remember, we will now focus on 'mix');
- Employee growth and development;
- Health and safety;
- Employee freedom, challenge, respect, and recognition.

All of these listed items are things a person can pursue in life without needing an organization. Placing ourselves in a position of requiring permission from an organization to have these things equates to an external locus of control. It suggests the organization has control over us.[36] It allows us to play the blame game if we don't get what we want out of life. Blame is simply an exercise in excuse-finding which equates to a refusal to manage. If we ourselves fall into this trap then what hope do we have of managing others away from it? If we blame in our own personal lives then odds are we will carry this behavior into the work setting – blaming people instead of working toward solutions.

---

[34] Full potential, for present purposes, will refer to full potential in all aspects of life and not just career aspects.

[35] Amy Cynkar: *Whole Workplace Health*. Monitor on Psychology, March 2007 Vol. 38 No. 3; Also: http://www.braintracy.com/blog/business-success/best-places-to-work-work-environment-business-ethics#ixzz2vqWTy7d4

[36] It's not that I hate organizations for what they are. Rather, I hate them for what they force us – as humans – to become: helpless, overly-reliant, incapable of picturing a reality full with their absence.

Four CommonPitfalls to a Plan

There are four dangers to managing our lives and I want to point them out now so as to ensure we do not stumble along the way.

The first, as you may have guessed, is having absolutely no plan or idea about life whatsoever. This can be life for a lot of people. The second is adhering too rigidly to a plan, allowing it to become bigger than you are, allowing it to cause golden opportunities to pass you by.[37] The third point to keep in mind is *Now*, right here, today. Freeing yourself from the past is great, planning for the future is sensible and mature, but don't miss the current moment.

The fourth danger I want to mention in relation to managing our lives is our tendency as humans to exaggerate the difficulty of achieving something *after* we have achieved it. Exaggerating the difficulty we have gone through is useful for pumping up our own self esteem, of introducing a positive self-talk (replacing "I can't" with "I can") and creating confidence for further challenges ahead. But the real problem comes when we hold others to those exaggerated standards rather than to the actual standards. This can lead to us becoming disappointed with others and others becoming unhappy in themselves.

Problems, Failure, Words, and Phrases

> We are so accustomed to faulty states of mind that it is difficult to change with just a little practice. Just a drop of something sweet cannot change a taste that is powerfully bitter. We must persist in the face of failure.[38]

---

[37] As you will come to see from exposure to organizational life, budgets often become ends in themselves; the main drivers of behavior, totally overshadowing objectives and leading to potentially massive problems.
[38] The Dalai Lama (2002) p. 37.

As a manager you must deal with problems and failure. You must learn to see them in context. Dealing with problems, failure, and the correct interpretation of words and phrases will enable you see a wider array of choices available thereby greatly enhancing your prospects for success.

Problems are a fact of life and business. We can limit them in number and effect, but we cannot eradicate them entirely. They must not become your barometer for life or managerial effectiveness. If you take a positive outlook then you can treat problems as opportunities. Problems don't arise for the heck of it. Problems don't think for themselves. They're not sadistic entities out to ruin your day. They are usually a sign you made an erroneous assumption, didn't factor something into your thinking, or couldn't possibly have foreseen what has just occurred. But for some reason we equate *problem* with *bad*. You quite simply cannot ever know everything. All change and strategy execution programs for example, however well planned, lead us into uncharted waters at some point. Taking the negative perspective in such instances really is self-defeating on so many levels.

"Failure" is another negatively viewed word. The overwhelming majority of us spend our lives afraid of it. We hold ourselves back and indulge in avoidance because of it. Again, just like problems, failure is a fact of life. It teaches us so many things if we allow it. Failure is not a reflection upon your true self-worth. If I fail on a project, I am the same person I was before I ever heard of that project. I will learn from the failure, analyze it to see what happened, talk with others about it to get their input. But I'm no less a human being because of it. Self-worth exists irrespective of my achievements or lack of achievements.

> ...Not to succeed in a particular endeavor is not to fail as a person. It is simply not being successful with that particular trial at that particular moment...Cats hunt mice; if they aren't successful in one attempt, they

simply go after another. They don't lie there and whine, complaining about the one that got away, or have a nervous breakdown because they failed.[39]

The *I can't* syndrome is one that ruins so many lives and careers and causes so many people to fall way short of their true potential. It is dangerous because it penetrates our internal programming without us even being aware of its presence. That quiet self-talk, that automatic response, destroys our chances before we even turn up at the starting line. Disempowering yourself makes little sense especially if you are looking to enter into the world of management. The *You Can't* fired at us by other people is also devastating. Incredibly, it tends to come our way during moments of doubt or crisis thereby greatly magnifying its effects. A lot of the time people don't even realize they are doing this to you. The subtle chipping away at our confidence by others is something you should become very alert to. Some people don't even mean to be negative. But little things do add up.

There are four harmful phrases to be alert to:

- That's me;
- I've always been that way;
- I can't help it;
- That's my nature.[40]

We can see a clear link between these and the two key phrases that haunt organizational life (as if seeking to prove that living is managing): *things will never change,* and, *we've always done it that way.* These six phrases have two things in common with things such as blame, guilt, worry, fear, and complaining. First, they are all phrases and behaviors we need to ditch if we are to become

---

[39] Dyer (1976) p. 132.
[40] Dyer (1976) p. 80

effective, successful, happy, content. Second, they are all forms of avoidance. When we speak the four phrases mentioned above, we are avoiding working on ourselves. The two organizational phrases will always be spoken by those terrified of change, with little imagination, with deep-seated comfort in the status quo.

Kill the Negativity

The first point on negativity we should be aware of is self-limiting beliefs (e.g. the I Can't Syndrome). These close our eyes to opportunities. They regulate the way in which we interpret everything around us. These beliefs have been programmed into us over the years by people around us and the world at large. And the majority of these self-limiting beliefs simply are not true. The business world demands that we step out of our comfort zones, take chances, risk failure. There are enough things in management acting as barriers without you adding to these by talking yourself down.

A second point on negativity is complaining. If instead, we shut-up for a while and thought about ways out of our problems, the world really would be such a better place. I like the following comment on people who complain too much:

> In extreme cases, they become "invisible"…When they enter a discussion, they are heard in silence, as if a pause button has been pressed; on finishing, the conversation resumes as though nothing has been added.[41]

A third point to look at when discussing negativity is the people around us. It is truly amazing just how massive an impact the people around you can have upon how successful and happy –

---

[41] Manzoni and Barsoux (2002) p. 118.

or not – you become (if you allow them).[42] Who are you surrounded by – at home and at work - on a regular basis? Do they lift you up or hold you down? This is important because studies show that emotions are contagious. Moods and emotions have also been shown to spread from the more expressive and vocal person to the more silent person. So in a room of pessimistic doubters, you don't stand much chance - get out!

And you'll have to deal with this when leading and managing people. Observing and listening for those who have an adverse effect upon others around them will become part of your daily routine. Dismissing people as cranks and crackpots, while ignoring their potential to cause serious damage, is not effective management. Identifying and isolating troublemakers is becoming a key skill.

But using the negativity of others is a very powerful technique put forward by Valerie Pierce in her short but brilliant book *Quick Thinking on Your Feet*. Pierce describes negative thinking as a fantastic knowledge base:

> When someone is pointing out the negatives as to why you can't achieve what you want, they are actually showing you how to get it. Listen to them...Once you know what the problem is you can concentrate on fixing it and getting what you want.[43]

---

[42] Be *very* careful here. Negative people does *not* equate to people with negative views – views contrary to yours. By negative people, we should have in mind those who drain our energy, our self-confidence, without any viable and worthy alternatives to suggest to us.
[43] Pierce (2003) p. 38. Pierce puts forward the idea that the reasons people give you when explaining why something is not possible actually point to how you can make it come about. Note also that Marcus Aurelius suggested such an approach: ..."for the mind converts and changes every hindrance to its activity into an aid; and so that which is a hindrance is made a furtherance to an act; and that which is an obstacle on the road helps us on this road" - Meditations, Part V, 20, p. 36.

Self-enforced negativity can also come about if we choose the wrong benchmarks against which to measure things. I have designed the following diagram to illustrate my point:

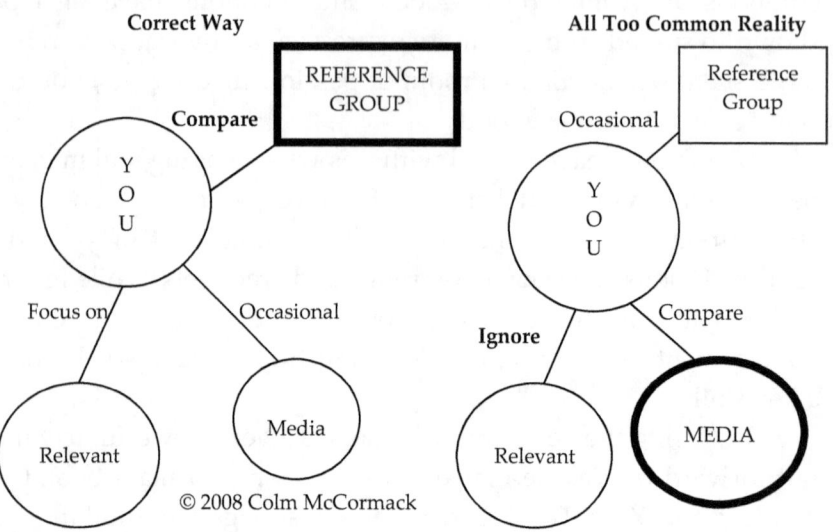

Under what I have labelled "The Correct Way" a person compares themselves to their reference group – their family; their sense of religion; the people better than them (on many fronts) that they aspire to emulate; their mentors - thereby focusing upon what is important. Under the "Reality" version of the model, however, far too many of us compare our looks, our spouses, our belongings, our houses, with those of fictional characters played by actors and actresses whose looks have been determined by genetics, surgery, or technology. This sees our reference group become less important to us thereby causing us to ignore the highly relevant aspects of our lives or, at worst, to see them as inferior and to then treat them in a way leading to unhappiness in ourselves and those around us.

Finally, moving away from negativity is one thing, but becoming an incurable optimist is not what you should be striving for.[44] You should seek to consider a problem, situation or person from as many different angles as possible. You must therefore take into account both the positive *and* negative information and operate from a position of realistic optimism. Sitting on a railway line admiring flowers and feeling highly positive and optimistic as the train speeds toward you won't stop you getting run over![45]

The BabySteps Concept

A lack of focus is very often the reason we come up short in life and in business. In considering your life plan you should decide what is *right* for you before you decide what is *possible*. If I tell you to plan to retire by the age of fifty, you will instantly decide to yourself that such a goal is impossible. That's because you're looking at where you are now and the finish line without looking at all the steps in between. Too many people make this mistake everyday. They focus on the start line, the finishing line, and conclude it's simply too fantastic and impossible a leap. In fact, people who do this should not be in management positions. It instantly reveals panic, an inability to plan, to look to the future. It also suggests an external locus of control, a failure to prioritize and a refusal to adopt a long-term perspective. This is where the concept I refer to as BabySteps comes in.

No matter what you're planning, break it down into small bite-sized and manageable chunks. The reality is that monthly, weekly, and daily steps, while seemingly unimportant in themselves, have a cumulative effect and are easily manageable.

---

[44] Various research over the years demonstrates that people with optimistic explanatory styles are less likely to develop health problems, are less likely to become depressed or suicidal, can have better academic and sports achievement, and can adjust better to bereavement and loss and occupational and family life situations. They have also been shown to have better chances of long-term marital satisfaction. See: Carr (2004) p. 84-85.

[45] Research has shown that positive coping self-statements are more effective than wishful positive thinking and self-affirmations. See: Scaturo (2005).

You've got to create regular short-term wins for yourself in order to maintain momentum. Take control. Give yourself every fighting chance. Use what Pierce refers to as the "great knowledge base" that negativity provides. Listen to why others (or yourself) are indicating you cannot achieve something and break all of these reasons into individual chunks to see ways around the problem: valuable negativity plus BabySteps operating in unison to provide workable solutions.[46] Buckets of unfocused energy will rarely beat a highly developed ability to plan, organize, and take action.

The Fat-Friday Method

I am not the worst eater you will ever meet. I'll be quite mindful of my diet throughout the week without being a health freak. But I'll eat whatever I feel like eating on a Friday – what I've come to call Fat Friday. And the idea is simple. The first time I did it, I gorged like a pig on Friday. Then after a few weeks, my stomach and system just couldn't take as much crap as previously – the six days to one ratio was starting to have an effect. After three or four months, Fat Friday saw me eating more or less exactly the same as any other day of the week.

And it's exactly the same when it comes to leading and managing. You *must* allow yourself relapses. You can't read this book and go from where you are now to fully effective in the blink of an eye. Your job is still there, so too are all the usual pressures of life. There are many distractions. So you start slowly. Do your best for a few days, then have your Fat Friday – the day when you don't beat yourself up for temporarily falling back into old habits. But over time, you'll notice your sense of self-worth, your conscience, etc, will start developing lower tolerances and won't take or issue as much nonsense as previously. This is the six days to one ratio

---

[46] Planning gives hope which builds resilience: all aided by the BabySteps method.

coming to your rescue. After a longer period of time (in truth it is a journey and never a destination) you'll find yourself acting more or less exactly the same on Fat Friday as any other day of the week. In other words, you'll start managing yourself thereby setting up justification for claiming you are becoming fit to lead and manage others.

The Five Constituency Model for Observing Behavioral Impact

I want to introduce you now to a model I have designed that will aid in your appreciation of managing yourself and, in time, of managing others. It will help you picture what is going on all around any person as they behave in any given way.

As you will see, the person under observation is placed at the heart of the diagram with firm lines of connection to and from the people around them, the organization, and external stakeholders. You, however, are slightly removed due to you exercising observation and therefore are not actively taking part or allowing yourself to be influenced by proceedings. The lines connecting you with the other four main constituencies are depicted as dashed to represent your awareness through observation of what is going on. In other words, you are aware and you choose what you will allow affect you and the extent of such affects. Take a look at the Five Constituencies diagram below:

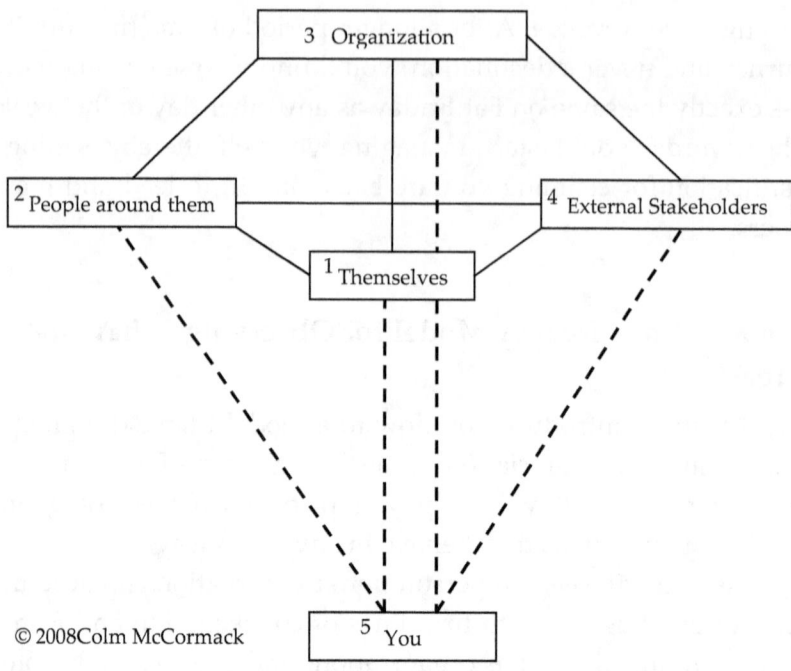

With this model/framework in mind, you would very briefly ask yourself various questions under each of the constituencies, for example:

Themselves	Can you get a feel for the perceptions, attitudes, etc, that are causing them to behave in the way they are? Might the absence of any real direction in their lives or trouble on the home front be the real cause? Are they blaming, complaining, refusing to take responsibility? Are they positive or negative? Do they seem trapped in a cycle?
People Around Them	How are those listening to them behaving and reacting? Is there a regular "audience" for these people?
Organization	Are there cliques popping up? Which is spreading the most throughout the organization: positive things or negative things? Where are the loyalties and do such loyalties transcend ranks?

External Stakeholders	What might outsiders think or say if they saw such behavior? I once sat waiting in the reception of a large organization while the two receptionists and a supervisor bitched openly about a manager without seeming to care who heard them.
You	But for the fact you are now watching, would you normally join in, get angry? Is not acting causing you to lose sleep at night? Are the actions or inactions of others intruding into your home life?

As an aid, use what I term the P.R.I.C.E. guidelines to keep issues of Paralysis, Reality, Inaction, Cowardice, and Ease of use in mind. See the table below:

Paralysis	This is not a paralysis-by-analysis model. Be brief. Simply pause to consider the five factors and then move on.
Reality	Dealing or not dealing with issues can see consequences seep out over time. Focusing only on the people in front of you misses the reality that people spread word of your action or inaction to the other constituencies.
Inaction	In a lot of cases, it is the *not* acting that can cause problems. Looking beyond the immediate person you are dealing with may instantly bring groups, cliques and coalitions to mind. The very act of considering Five Constituencies, and not just two should give you a fuller picture of the context in which you are standing.
Cowardice	Focusing on cliques and coalitions should not become a license for cowardice. The entire point behind looking briefly at all Five Constituencies is not that you choose inaction: it is that you choose suitable and effective action that will contain effects from seeping out to external stakeholders and others.[47]
Ease	Simplicity and genius usually walk hand-in-hand. This is a fast and easy to use model. It should give you a broader picture, expand the range of areas within your consideration and move you toward more suitable and informed decisions and/or actions.

---

[47] Stakeholders for present purposes refers to customers, suppliers, distributors, strategic partners, investors, the bank manager – everyone outside the organization you should be thinking of because they are thinking of you; parties who can hurt you if you shake their confidence.

The point of the Five Constituency Model is to enable you to:

- Avoid the "False Reality" problem;[48]
- Expand the range of Choices available to you;
- Develop big picture thinking;
- Take effective and targeted action that contains its own impacts from spreading out to other constituencies;
- Prevent you causing further damage.

The Five Constituencies and Dealing with Eddie

Eddie has been causing problems for a while now. His team members have made several remarks to him but these have all gone ignored. Eddie is too relaxed and this is putting the team on edge. Everyone around him is uptight because they never know when he will start his work and the type of quality they might expect from him. Most of his team have stopped talking to him except when really necessary.

Eddie, on the other hand, always gets his work done on time. He feels that if the others are worrying about his performance then that is *their* problem. He doesn't feel he has to hop to it when the others say and he doesn't feel he should do things their way. He has mentioned to one or two other workers in other parts of the organization that his team members are jerks and panic junkies.

You now have to deal with this situation. Brian, the Team Leader, has come to you because you as manager are the only one with the power to fire people. Brian feels that Eddie is undermining him since a showdown between them simply sees Eddie sitting back and smiling because he knows that Brian can't do anything more than have a few words with him. The other members of the

---

[48] Mistakingly seeing the reality of the situation you are in as consisting only of you and the person before you. Explained further in the coming pages.

team have mentioned to Brian in private that he should come to see you and this is making him feel belittled and disempowered.

Five minutes after Brian talking with you and returning to his desk you see Eddie behaving like a bit of a jerk. Right at this moment you can see only three options open to you: let fly at Eddie, shout in Eddie's direction to come into your office right now, or fire Eddie on the spot.

Let us assume you reacted by using one of these options. We can briefly summarize the managerial mistakes you make as follows:

Emotional Stability	You have become emotionally involved and have reacted emotionally. The outburst from out of nowhere is unbecoming of a mature and responsible manager.
Locus of Control	It is Eddie's behavior that is now controlling your emotions and not you. In your mind, Eddie is "making" you angry. You need to take control back from Eddie and adopt an Internal Locus of Control.
Interpersonal Skills	Your interpersonal skills have fallen in perceived quality since there was a total absence of tact, consideration, and sensitivity. You charged in thinking only of Eddie and his behavior and exploded on front of everybody around him.
"Problem"	Seeing this Problem as a threat rather than an opportunity is short sighted. You should have reframed to ensure a more sensible and suitable approach.

Let us now view the scenario before us via the lens of the Five Constituency Model. But remember, you are not out to manage Eddie here. It's too easy to make that mistake. You are concentrating on managing *You* at this point.[49]

---

[49] Managing others comes in The 'PEOPLE' Factor – the second book in the series. Go to: www.JustManageIt.guru for further details.

The 'YOU' Factor

Constituency 1 - Eddie	What do you know about him? Does he sulk? Is he reasonable to talk to? What age is he? How long has he been here? Is his future here or is this a stop-gap or stepping-stone? Asking yourself these questions about Eddie gets you to focus on him and not on his behavior. Looking beyond his behavior allows you to remain calm, to detach.
Constituency 2 - the People around Eddie: his team members	They have clearly had enough of this. They bitch and moan privately to each other and to Brian but will not speak with Eddie as a group. We might even say that an inability in Brian to manage himself now sees his team controlling him in addition to Eddie's behavior controlling him too. Now you are starting to think more deeply about the matter and should be a long way from exploding emotionally: your heart has been disengaged and your brain engaged.
Constituency 3 - the Organization as a whole	We know that this is getting around the building because Eddie has commented to others in different departments. So this problem is no longer contained. And yet you might have missed this had you not used the Five Constituency model when assessing the problem. Instead, all you might have seen was Eddie needing to have his ass kicked. You need to know who these others are, their positions and titles, etc, to ensure your action keeps them isolated and the matter contained.
Constituency 4 - the External Stakeholders.	You don't know whether or not this problem has seeped out to touch this constituency. But there is the sharp possibility that outsiders are aware of something not being right even if only from throw away remarks or vague references in telephone conversations. It is therefore crucial that your behavior does not exacerbate the situation.
Constituency 5 - You.	You were about to storm out the door and deal with Eddie. Whatever about the merits of allowing people to push you into acting, you should not allow them to dictate your *style* of acting. Now you are emotionally removed from the situation. You can observe from a distance. It is now you who controls your emotions. You can retain emotional stability. You can learn. You can avoid lowering the perceived quality of your interpersonal skills. You can see how this is impacting on all constituencies and therefore plan an effective and suitable intervention that will contain the issue and prevent it from seeping out any further to Constituencies 3 & 4.

I want you to become mindful of what I term the "False Reality" problem: seeing the reality of the situation as simply involving you and the person you are focused on – in this case Eddie. The *actual* reality is that all Five Constituencies are watching and listening – so you must act accordingly to avoid later managing the consequences of your own misguided interventions.

Previously, in our example involving Eddie, you may have simply fired him. And you might do exactly the same now except with the Five Constituency model in mind you will act from a position of managing yourself properly and ensuring that the action you take is contained from constituencies 3 & 4 – the rest of the Organization and the External Stakeholders - and that constituency 2 – the People Around Him - is not given any reason to spread gossip to 3 & 4. The point *must* be clear: you need to know how to manage yourself first *before* you can manage others in anything approaching an *effective* way. Managing yourself does not mean you become a wimp or a doormat. Instead, you will act with considered purpose and in an effective self-managed way.

Looking at You

Look at the main areas of your life: work, family, health, finances, and personal time/hobbies/interests. What needs improvement? Start planning for the future across all areas, i.e. start to get a Life Plan together. Keep it simple. You're not out to change the world or turn it on its head. Within reason, focus on what you want and *not* what you think is possible. The BabySteps process will rescue you here. Determine what you want and then break everything down into small chunks and timelines to turn the plan into a realistic and possible journey.[50] Remember; *all* parts of your

---

[50] For greater description on how to construct a Life Plan, I highly recommend you visit the website and books of Brian Tracy. See: www.briantracyinternational.com

life must stay in focus and not backslide out of the picture because of work pressures or poor personal discipline.

How do you define "problem", "failure", and "rejection"? Are you happy with your definitions? Next, ask yourself the following questions.

- Do you complain a lot? If so, why? How difficult would it be for you to stop complaining?
- Do you have any negative people around you? How are they affecting you?
- Can you tell the difference between negative people and people bringing you negative news?
- Both at home and at work, do you have the correct reference group in mind? Go back and look at the diagram I drew on this point to refresh your memory.[51]
- Start a Success Diary. Keep a note of your daily wins and successes. Review it regularly to put things into perspective and combat negative thoughts, stress, etc.[52]

Begin to observe the people around you. See if you can determine the effect they are having on the Five Constituencies. Try to get a feel for the bigger picture rather than simply looking at the person him/herself. You are trying to develop the habit of wider and more complete thinking. And remember, you're just observing. In time, watching others will cause you to start regulating yourself. When you see people being negative or gossiping, you'll also notice when you yourself start behaving that way. With negativity,

---

[51] Correct reference group should never be taken to mean hampering your ability to improve. There is nothing that says mixing with people who are more successful and better connected than you equates to mixing in the wrong group. The meaning that is to be taken is that you should avoid mixing with fickle people whose standards lead to personal unhappiness.
[52] Also useful for combating the development of a McGregor Theory X outlook. See following footnote.

internal locus of control, etc all on your mind, you'll start to spot them everywhere. Watch for the positives too. [53]

Later, we will invert the Five Constituency diagram to get a feel for how *your* behavior impacts upon others. Until then, simply recognize that you've been looking at the world all your life – now it's time to starting *seeing* it. Management is a human activity. Start watching humans!

Some Final Thoughts

Before managing others it is crucial that you are capable of managing yourself. Not doing so will simply see you create unnecessary problems for yourself and for others. If you are prone to emotional outbursts, cannot admit mistakes, cannot see yourself as part of both the problem and the solution, have poor interpersonal skills, suffer from anger, addiction, have an external locus of control – and all the other things we have touched on so far – then you are not managing yourself as effectively as you should. There is no need to sit some fancy psychological test. You already know how you score on such issues. Be honest with yourself. Think of what a nightmare such managers are for their employees. We've all seen terrible managers like this. Nobody likes having to work with or for them.

The solution to this predicament is quite simple. It only takes a little time and thought. We will work through it as we make our way from chapter to chapter. But already you know of the need to ditch blame and take responsibility for the here-and-now and the future both at home and at work. Move toward an internal locus of

---

[53] Or you run the risk of converting yourself to a McGregor Theory X type mindset in which workers are viewed as being lazy, as requiring to be coerced, as shying away from responsibility and needing to be controlled. Micro-managing, by the way, is often referred to as owning a dog but barking yourself! It can also see you turning experts from forces for positive momentum into rocks to be dragged.

control. Move away from all the forms of negative thinking we looked at, the people who hold you back and start adopting a better perspective on things such as failure and problems. Plot objectives across a wide mix of areas in life and not just in business. Start managing. You're not out to become a dangerous and incurable optimist but you are seeking a better perspective and a better approach. Managing is a verb, an action word, so be proactive, determined, and realistic. When you are happy so too are those around you - at home and at work.

Chapter 2
Constantly Reassess

Toward Creating the Psychological Default Setting

> A bad researcher uses research in much the same way a drunk uses a lamppost: for support and not illumination.[54]

Everything we have looked at so far in ourselves and in others will see us reassessing many life-long habits, perceptions, perspectives. Now, in order to move toward becoming effective managers, we will look at making reassessment constant, natural, and beneficial; for people who lead and manage must always aim to see things as they *actually* are and not as we think they are or accept them to be.

You must therefore develop the ability to reassess constantly and naturally *especially* during times of pressure, crisis, and emergency.

Nietzsche and Bacon Were On to Something!

Doubt is the enemy of faith. We know this to be true because by doubting something we are caused to investigate, to explore, to discover, to question. The word "enemy" is very carefully chosen here by those fearful of change. But this particular "enemy" *must* be

---

[54] This is a quotation I picked up in my early teenage years and has been with me ever since. My apologies to whoever penned it. I quite simply do not know their identity.

welcomed with open arms. In a world in which nothing is static it is our duty to doubt: a duty imposed by our need for survival and our desire for improvement.

In so many ways the worlds of business and management have allowed models, philosophies, approaches – the everyday way of seeing, believing, and doing things – to take on positions of existence similar to beliefs held within the religious context. We take certain things as golden rules. We may not even know why we believe such things – as with religion – we simply believe them: we have faith in the absence of any tangible proof. Friedrich Nietzsche, at two different points in his work *The Gay Science* makes the following pertinent observations:

> ...the vast majority do not find it contemptible to believe this or that, and to live in accordance with this belief without first being aware of the ultimate and securest reasons for and against it and without afterwards even taking the trouble to discover such reasons – the most gifted men and the noblest women are still among this 'vast majority' ...they feel, rather, a thirst for things which are contrary to reason and do not put too many difficulties in the way of satisfying it.

We must remember at all times our new philosophy: *Living is* Managing. Therefore, taking what Nietzsche has indicated here, we see that *things have always been done that way*, and, *that will never change*, are comments confined not to the world of work in isolation, but to life in general. You will also remember the four sentences we encountered in the Get a Life chapter (That's me, I've always been that way, I can't help it, that's my nature). We can strengthen our understanding of the *need* for a principle of Constantly Reassess by heeding the warnings sounded by Francis Bacon. In pointing out the things that can lead man astray, Bacon warned about:

- The desire to accept that which confirms what we already know;
- Distortions resulting from our habitual ways of thinking;
- Muddles that come through our use of language;
- Believing things out of an allegiance to a particular school of thought.[55]

If we didn't know better, we would label Bacon a management guru. His points really are so pertinent to the world of work with which we are all familiar.

Bad Habits

Not activating Constantly Reassess is simply a bad habit developed over years. Not exercising proper control of our attitudes, and perspectives - thereby maintaining the status quo - is simply a position that keeps the Constantly Reassess in all of us dormant and capable of activating in only the most unusual and alarming of circumstances. A habit can be defined as:

> An acquired behavior pattern regularly followed until it has become almost involuntary.

Constantly Reassess suggests that we *un*-acquire ineffective patterns of behavior and replace them with desirable patterns that become – in the ideal – almost involuntary. And that is what we must aim for.

> Remember, bad habits are *easy* to form, but hard to live with; good habits are *hard* to form, but easy to live with. Your job is to form good habits and make them your masters.[56]

---

[55] Thompson (1995) p. 40
[56] Tracy (1993) p. 91.

Imagine you are a subway worker and a train pulls up to the platform during morning rush hour. You are there to ensure the trains run on time. The doors open and people burst out onto the platform coughing, vomiting and collapsing into unconsciousness. Would you clear the carriage of people and then send the train on its way in order to keep the rush hour trains on time? Would you think there was something wrong with the carriage or in the tunnel? What if on another train your colleagues remove two suspect passages, two unconscious people, and others coughing? Do you think at any time you should reassess your focus of keeping the trains running on time? These very events and actions occurred on the Tokyo underground during a morning rush hour Sarin attack in March of 1995. It seems incredible now, but the pressure to keep trains running on time meant that unconscious people and suspect packages were cleared by hand and the trains sent on their way to fill up with more people. Or imagine willingly walking to your death and ignoring an opportunity to escape. This happened many times during the Second World War to Jewish prisoners.

But keep it simple and everyday if you like. Let's say the media tell you that road deaths in your area are, for example, up to three hundred and fifty from two hundred and ninety last year. Instantly you will think, uh-oh, that's bad. But wait a minute. Rather than jumping for the statistics, reassess what you are hearing with questions such as:

- Might there be more cars on the road (car sales up due to economic boom)?
- Has the weather been worse this summer/winter than last year?
- Are there more immigrants or tourists driving on the streets this year?
- Have demographic issues come into play, i.e. has there been a large wave of people reaching legal driving age this year?

Do the same in work. If you are told a particular worker is causing problems, ask yourself some insightful questions before diving into action. For example:[57]

Timing	How long has this been a problem?
Magnitude	How big is the problem/the effects?
Antecedents	What led up to the problem?
Scope	Did the problem occur with others too?

Not asking yourself these questions can see you fall prey to devious organizational politics, failing to recognize that someone may not have been managing an ongoing problem, failing to eliminate the causes of this problem in the future and lining yourself up for bullying and harassment suits through inconsistent actions.

Don't make the mistake of viewing critical thinking as negative complaining-type thinking. Critical in this sense refers to looking at the conclusions objectively and then digging behind them to see what they have been based upon – reassessing.

As we saw, tragedy arriving on a subway platform was ignored because the workers were so intent on meeting targets. If something that obvious presents itself, what chance do workers have if something less obvious occurs? What if people in your company are so focused on meeting targets that crucial developments, stale perspective, faulty mindsets, go unnoticed? The failure to activate Constantly Reassess can present problems so severe that people have been shown to walk willingly to extermination due to its absence.

---

[57] See Yukl (2006).

Your Chessboard of Competence

Think of your life, both at and away from work, as a giant chess board. All of the squares on the board are deep. In these squares sit ice cubes that sit down level with the surface of the board. The board, however, is warm so that the ice cubes melt and the water drips out through grills beneath. The squares are the areas of your personal and working life, for example, one square might represent "conflict", another "financial analysis", another "personal health", etc. The ideal situation is always to have a full ice cube in each square. Not doing so produces "dips" in the otherwise level surface of the board. Dips cause you to stumble!

In terms of your working life, the more volatile and dynamic the industry in which you work, the hotter the squares. In other words, your ice cubes melt faster. Therefore, your ice cubes represent your cutting edge, effective, and pertinent knowledge in each of the labelled squares. So, if for example, I work in the IT sector, there is every likelihood that neglecting to keep my knowledge of, say, wire-free technology, fully up-to-date, will cause me harm. In other words, that particular square may be very hot thereby melting my knowledge into irrelevance and causing me to stumble upon the I.T. path. The dip represents a lack of new knowledge. The stumble comes when I present *old* knowledge as the solution to any *new* situation.

The opposite will be the case in a stagnant industry, or in an area of life at which I excel. A colder square means less work since the ice cubes melt slower (if at all). But we must be careful not to fall asleep in our chair: a regular and thorough inspection of all squares is required since heat will arise *under* the ice, i.e. we will not necessarily see the arrival of the need until our knowledge, expertise, or fitness in that square has already been eroded.

Constantly Reassess is Taught at Trinity

This idea of Constantly Reassess is nothing new. It is all around us but under different labels. In the religious context, for example, there is the familiar concept of setting aside some time at the end of the day to be quiet and to reflect on the thoughts that occurred to you and that arose from incidents during the day. By reflecting upon them, assessing your attitude and perspective, you ensure everything is in check with your beliefs, etc.

Take note of the following attitude:

> ...the daily work of each person sowing seeds for the future will eventually contribute to the creation of heaven or hell.[58]

What an interesting way, if we borrow this line from its original context, to look at management and the presence or absence of Constantly Reassess. Without the principle, we have the potential to create hell both in the world in which we live and at work. Not constantly reassessing can lead to those two awful enemies of management surfacing: "things have always been done that way", and, "things will never change". On the contrary, however, use of Constantly Reassess gives us, at the very least, the *potential* to create a better business and home life (heaven) or to at least avoid allowing them become bad ones (hell).

This idea of reflection is exactly what dozens of students engage in every day at Trinity College, Dublin. There, MSc Counseling Psychology students will have group and one-to-one reflection sessions (in addition to their own mandatory counseling). They will discuss their problems, discuss what they said, discuss how they felt during sessions, etc. In essence, Constantly Reassess is alive and well on the Trinity MSc program. Only by reflecting upon the day's or week's events can the students ever hope to learn, to

---

[58] Okawa (2002) p. 155

overcome personal biases, prejudices, attribution errors. It is long past time to awaken this activity and approach within the Business and Management Schools of the world.[59] Does it exist in *your* organization?

Constantly Reassess in Work

In any organization top managers can find themselves locked within their departmental patterns of thinking and therefore incapable of developing an effective corporate view.[60] To avoid falling into this kind of trap, you should always Constantly Reassess things such as:

- The Demands made of you, the Constraints under which you are operating, and the Choices you have made, are making, and will make;
- The way in which you use your time;
- The quality of the people around you;
- Your information, analysis, and decisions;
- Your motives, objectives, and goals;
- Has your ego stepped in and taken over?
- The processes and systems in place;
- The feedback or lack of it from various sources, especially from customers, suppliers, and employees on the frontlines
- Are you helping the competition?
- Are you squeezing the wrong people e.g. good suppliers and vendors (because of your low-cost strategy, for example)?

---

[59] You will notice this specific point of personal and group counseling was missing from chapter one. It is most certainly crucial and something we will return to later. But for now, I can tell you that the simple issues covered so far, with discussion and reflection, are very effective.
[60] Belbin (2004)

- Ar you training staff to leave?
- Does your company see itself as invulnerable?
- What business are you really in?
- Are you growing too fast?
- Do you over-promise but under-deliver?

I am not advocating paralysis-by-analysis. What I am advocating, however, is a willingness to accept: you may be wrong, ill-informed, subject to ego, on the wrong road. Too many of us need to wake-up in our own jobs: familiarity does indeed breed contempt.

> Be suspicious of things that you don't understand, and even more suspicious if someone explains them to you and you still don't understand...If there is something you are unhappy or unclear about, keep coming back to it: probe, ask questions, be intellectually honest.[61]

Constantly Reassess in Personal Life

Your Life Plan which we discussed in Chapter 1 will take in both the organizational and personal life aspects that should be subject to Constantly Reassess. Go back to your Life Plan regularly. Watch out for your assumptions!

We have already hit upon Locus of Control and so many other things such as positivity, proactivity, etc. But in looking at our own situations as people, Greenberger and Padesky[62] detail an interesting approach to dealing with personal issues. They indicate there are five aspects to our life experiences. These are:

- Our thoughts;
- Our moods;
- Our behaviors;

---

[61] Robinson (2004) Pg. 182
[62] (1995).

- Our physical reactions;
- And the environment in which we find ourselves.

The fantastic thing about their approach is that a change in any one of these aspects can affect all of the others.[63] So if, for example, I change the way in which I think about a problem that has been getting me down (I've Reassessed), my mood in relation to this problem will change for the better, my behavior will become more proactive and positive, my physical reactions will be those of a happier and more determined person, and the environment around me will change by, for example, others being drawn to interact with and assist me. In other words, Constantly Reassess can lead me to look at any of the five aspects, and my strong internal locus of control will bring about different outcomes in so much more than just the one aspect I focused on at the start.

Let us now revisit the Five Constituencies and look at the *Inverted* version of the model:

---

[63] Just as change in one S of the 7-S framework in strategy sees an impact of varying degrees upon the remaining six S's – See Mullins (2005). The 7-S's are: Systems, Style, Strategy, Structure, Staff, Skills and Superordinate goals. A change in systems, for example, will see a change in operating style, a need to retrain staff, change skills and style, etc. In other words, changing one can lead to a change in all the others.

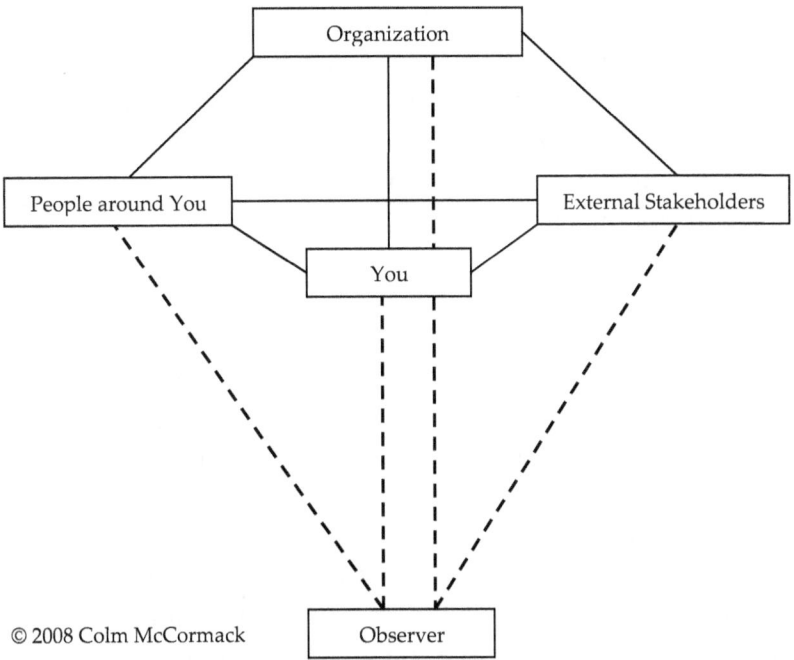

Note how YOU are now the center of observational attention and another person has sat into the position of observation. This should enable you to gain an insight into the ways in which your own behavior affects so much more around you than is usually in your contemplation. Would all others view you favorably? Again, revisit the example questions detailed earlier when introducing the model and answer them about yourself as asked by someone who is observing you.

Remember; at this point keep it brief. The whole idea is to get you to think beyond simply you and the person you are dealing with. Make sure the actions you take or don't take enable you to contain fall-out from spreading to external stakeholders and the organization as a whole.

Constantly Reassess really is one of the most important principles you will ever encounter in life and in business. It is almost like the butterfly flapping its wings in Tokyo causing a tidal wave in San Francisco: a simple reassessment of one small aspect of your daily life (behavior, thoughts, attitudes, reactions,) can have a disproportionately massive benefit in so many other things. And a lot of the time it's more than just you who benefits – great leadership and management!

The REAL Enemy

According to Stephen Schiffman[64] the real enemy in business is the status quo. The status quo here is something we will take as referring to our thoughts, attitudes, perspectives, beliefs. So if we allow all of these things to stay the same from year to year without questioning then we increase our chances of failure. Self-awareness and continuous self-development and improvement are becoming the order of the day. Without them, we not only fall behind; we fail to achieve our true potential. But these things never even hit the radar screen if our inbuilt Constantly Reassess is never activated.

So we must activate it. Only by working consciously on ourselves will it become accustomed to use. Using it in one context will, by small degrees, cause it to activate in other areas of our working day. If, for example, I am monitoring my tendency to be defensive or critical, I will spot such behavior in others. Defensiveness in others (and other reactions) can aid us in regulating our own behavior.

Reframing

While writing this book, buses would pass me regularly around the streets of Dublin, Ireland with adverts by mobile phone

---

[64] Schiffman. (2003).

giant Vodafone. They would state things like: "This is not a bus, it's a place to talk", or, "This is not a street, it's an office".

The ability to reframe – to see the same circumstances in a different light – is crucial for effective managers. This is because we are all products of our past experiences. We arrive into situations with pre-determined ways of seeing and interpreting things, whether we realize it or not. Numbers people, for example, will see numbers problems and will adopt numbers solutions. In other words, by virtue of our past experiences, we are generally very limited in our outlook.

None of this should be new to us. We have already entertained the idea of reframing perceived problems as opportunities. For example:

> 'I can't go for that job, I am too old (assumption old is bad) *change this* to 'I can go for that job, as I have a wealth of experience' (old is good).[65]

The treatment of psychological trauma will often see a counsellor or therapist attempting to get, for example, an abused child, to move from a sense of victimization to one of survivorship in the personal narratives of their lives. In other words, by reframing they can draw on the benefits rather than becoming immobilized.[66]

We know that failing to sell something is not a rejection of us as people: we can reframe it for what it is – a rejection of the product or service we are offering. The trick, of course, is to reach a point where reframing comes naturally, or at least the recognition of the need to reframe. Instead of thinking "Will I make it?" start thinking, "*How* will I make it?"[67] A very simple stop and reframe. As soon as you question your ability to do something *that* is the

---

[65] Pierce (2003) p. 76
[66] See: Scaturo (2005).
[67] Positive, proactive, creative.

need to reframe surfacing right there. It is when reframing doesn't come naturally or never occurs to our busy minds that the problems arise.

How many times have you passed someone and thought, "Scumbag" because of their appearance? How many "idiots" do you encounter? What about the guy in the expensive suit – what's your label for him? We stick these labels on people without even hearing them speak: we just pass them in the street. It is only when such labelled people act contrary to the label - the comedian getting violent, the thug helping the woman with her groceries - that we see the need to reframe. Unfortunately, however, most of the contrary behavior is not seen or only seen by a small number of people. So the label sticks.[68] This is dangerous in business as well as in personal life. From the first meeting at interview right the way through to sales, negotiations - everything – we stick labels on people and immediately limit our room to manoeuvre as a result.

In business, an ability to reframe a cost as an *investment* can make the world of difference. Reframing your more expensive product or service as more efficient, longer lasting, can be highly beneficial in a sales scenario. But you won't do any of this unless you prepare and unless you see the need and opportunity to reframe. This is why Constantly Reassess is one of the most important principles in this book: unless your mind is silently on guard in the background, you'll miss so much and only see narrow segments of the full picture before you. You'll condemn yourself to dealing with half-options, dealing with symptoms rather than causes, dealing with the how and not the why.

---

[68] Labeling certainly helps us to make sense of the world around us but we are labeling far too much. It has reached the point where our labeling mania is hurting us. We are interpreting too many things incorrectly. How do instant labels such as "babe", "fox", "scumbag" etc, that spring to mind as people pass us in the street benefit us? Bias, prejudice, dislike, rush to judgment, etc, have us seeing the wrong things, expecting the wrong things, reacting in the wrong way, and therefore managing the wrong things.

The Criteria

> ...whether awake or asleep, we ought never to allow ourselves to be persuaded of the truth of anything unless on the evidence of our reason. And it must be noted that I say of our *reason,* and not of our imagination or of our senses.[69]

You will remember our little story in the introduction about my uncles installing the patio doors. This little story now gives us two criteria for our principle of Constantly Reassess.

First, the assumption about the foundations. Just how long does it take to check they are level? Probably about ten seconds or so. Second, how come the original builder never spotted that his brick work was off beam? Constantly Reassess means that at intervals, as the wall rose in height, he would have checked to ensure nothing new had occurred to undermine the quality of his work. So here we have two situations in which the principle should be used: at the start and at regular intervals throughout.

Now we are starting to see the emergence of the criteria for Constantly Reassess:

- It is not Brainstorming;
- It may initiate Brainstorming;
- It may inform, question, correct, judge, and sustain Brainstorming;
- It should occur at the start of any process;
- It should occur at intervals throughout each process;
- It may even be responsible for starting any process in the first place;
- It must come into use *especially* when time is tight, when the pressure is on, and during times of crisis and emergency.

---

[69] Descartes (1637, 2004) Part IV, p. 36.

The building blocks of the Constantly Reassess process are depicted in the diagram below:

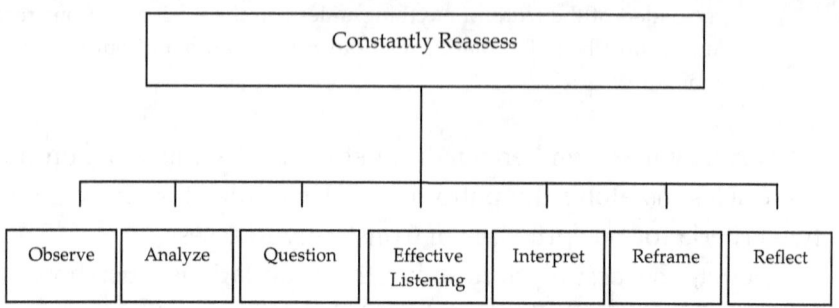

© 2008 Colm McCormack

We are already familiar with some of the labels here; for example, observe, reframe, reflect. The remaining labels will be explained and become familiar to you as we proceed through the book.

Creating the Default Setting

So how do you get Constantly Reassess to occur naturally as your psychological default setting? Furthermore, how do you get your workers to this position so that everybody in the organization is sharp, alert, on top of their game?

In a way, a healthy disrespect, a critical approach, a willingness not to be a fool, is what is called for. One Irish newspaper had a fantastic motto: *"Questions answered – answers questioned"*.[70] In the information age and the knowledge economy it would be the highest level of naivety to assume information and knowledge are not manipulated, misinterpreted, used out of

---

[70] The Sunday Tribune. See: www.tribune.ie

context or just downright incorrect. Hence the urgency to acquire and utilize Constantly Reassess.

Merely advocating people in your organization Constantly Reassess is not enough. Simple dictates ignore the complexities of the human mind and the way in which it perceives and interprets situations. More importantly, it highlights the need to train managers to recognize that an ability to momentarily disengage from a situation, especially when pressure starts to build (e.g. Tokyo underground Sarin attack), is essential.

Unless people are placed in situations, filmed/recorded, and then subjected to 360 degree feedback,[71] management is not a skill that will emerge efficiently. Leaving matters entirely in the hands of Experience is not the right answer either.[72]

But Constantly Reassess is something that can come from on the job coaching. Watching ourselves, or self-awareness, is the starting point. We can then teach others to watch their own behavior, get them to explore their thoughts, perspectives, etc. Better yet, others watching us break down organizationally determined social inhibitions – questioning, debating, confronting – can lead to what I term *Positive Social Contagion*[73] whereby our positive practice constitutes leading by good example. To unleash it in an entire organization, however, requires time. As we will see later in Chapter 9, *Everybody* Sets an Example – and it is the desired example we are looking to create via the snowball effect of positive social contagion.

---

[71] I am not a fan of 360 Degree feedback in the organizational setting. More often than not, it presents itself as dishonest, subject to pre-determined budgetary constraints, and is rendered impotent in the face of loyalty among employees to each other. In small groups yes, but in large organizations (many perform the feedback through emails) it is both impractical and unsuitable.

[72] Experience can take too long, be expensive, demands that you make mistakes, can teach you the wrong things, and can create a one-fits-all solution mentality.

[73] See section entitled: *Spread Positivity like Wildfire*, Chapter 9.

Portfolio and Job Rotation

One of the best ways to reawaken Constantly Reassess in the working environment is via portfolio and job rotation. A very simple example of portfolio rotation would be taking your list of clients and handing it to the guy beside you and then giving you his clients. The idea is to keep workers interested, keep them sharp and on their toes. If I take it a step further and rotate staff from department to department (job rotation), then I give workers a broader and more general set of skills. It also gives them a better understanding of how the organization operates as a whole – something that is useful in avoiding unnecessary inter-departmental conflict. In other words, they start to reassess previously held assumptions. If they are shifted around on a regular basis, this reassessment becomes constant – Constantly Reassess becomes the norm.

Japanese production companies are renowned for rotating employees from task to task. Studies of Japanese companies using rotation have shown a high degree of trust between managers and employees, a sharing in the decision making process, and a strong sense of collective responsibility for the faith of the organization. Jason Jennings,[74] in his number one selling book *Less is More*,[74] deals with this topic in a very interesting way. He indicates that portfolio rotation (the white collar version of rotation where clients, accounts, files, geographical areas, etc are moved around staff members) is highly effective if rotation occurs every eighteen months or so. Veteran magazine publisher and entrepreneur Felix Dennis also discovered the benefits from many years of experience and says:

> You will get the most out of any senior employee in their first year or two in a new position. After that, they enter a 'comfort zone'.[75]

---

[74] Jennings (2002).
[75] Dennis (2007) p. 257.

I experienced portfolio rotation myself in the insurance world when a new team structure was introduced. Getting new clients suddenly put us on our toes, but it did the same for the clients and lawyers too. New faces, new attitudes, a willingness to impress – all these things kicked in. Everyone inside the organization and all the people we dealt with on the outside started to reassess. Since then, I have been convinced that rotating portfolios, files, clients, is one of the best things managers can do. Of course, not everyone is convinced. Comfort and change can cause bizarre excuses to surface as creatures of habit fight to retain the status quo. Remember; money is a great attractor but over time becomes a poor retainer. Challenge, excitement, achievement, recognition, personal growth – these are the things that retain top talent. Portfolio and job rotation offer all those things. And when your top talent is happy and working, the organization is on the road to success.

Let me, however, sound one important warning. Rotating people and portfolios may lead to an initial drop in performance. This is only natural. It takes a while for people to get up to speed with a new task. Does such a delay cost you a lot of money (what is the opportunity cost of rotation)? It shouldn't. It's only when you do something idiotic like tell the entire accounts department to stand up and swap with I.T. and I.T. to swap with marketing that real trouble starts. As a sensible human being, you will carry rotation out in a measured way so as to limit any potential adverse effects. In managing yourself, don't be afraid to seek rotation as a form of professional development.

Some Final Thoughts

Developing an inbuilt default ability akin to shouting, "Stop!" or "Trick!" or "What's wrong with this picture!?" is of vital importance if you are seeking to manage yourself effectively thereby setting you up to lead and manage others. There is so much truth in the idea that the quality of our lives – both at home and at work - depends upon the quality of the questions we ask.

Mistakes are and will continue to be made everyday; you will never have all the information you need or all the time you would like. Of crucial importance, is the ability to get out of your own way - remember; most of any manager's problems emanate from that manager him/herself. You cannot ever hope to improve unless you are willing to accept you will always require ongoing improvement; ongoing improvement demands the ability to constantly reassess your own mood, attitude, perspective, energy level, feelings, thinking, experience, information coming to you, the people around you – and more.

Observing others can be a wonderful self-regulation technique: the mistakes made by others can make us aware of such behaviour in ourselves; the opposite is also true: watch those who are succeeding and notice when such behaiors are absent from your own repertoire.

A failure to entertain and engage in the idea that, to be successful as a person and when seeking to lead and manage others, you must develop an inbuilt default ability to Constantly Reassess, will see blame shift or migrate to you for the poor and resulting consequences. This idea of blame migrating is where we are headed to next in Chapter 3.

Chapter 3
All Blame Migrates

> If turnover is down, profits are down, orders are down, new customers are few, and your direct competitors are doing better than you are – then, for heaven's sake, don't ignore this. Don't blame it on the market or someone else; acknowledge that you have a problem [76]...The golden rule is: the moment you first suspect that there may be a problem with a member of staff, a product, a part of the service you offer, a geographical area or a department, investigate immediately. Never, never put it off. As in health, small problems left unattended grow into big problems. Tackle it now![77]

All Blame Migrates - sooner or later. Imagine someone is lazy while you do all the work. Going ballistic in front of your spouse when you get home is understandable but only for a limited period of time. After a while, not confronting the particular employee or going higher up the chain of command allows the blame to migrate from the lazy employee to *you*. Lawyers will be very familiar with this concept. When you are on notice of someone causing you loss but you fail to act to limit that loss, instead pointing the finger of blame at others, eventually *you* will be penalized for failing to mitigate your own loss.

The Smoking Gun Syndrome

We have all watched the old movies where the unfortunate woman is found in the library standing over the victim with a smoking gun in her hand. To everyone in the movie it is such an

---

[76] Robinson (2004) pg. 92
[77] Robinson (2004) pg. 113

open and shut case. The victim is there, the murder weapon is there, the shots were heard just moments ago – who else could it have been?

You must bear in mind that blame is a very gregarious creature: it loves company. Systems, processes, procedures – all of these things – may attract attention when things go wrong. In other words, secondary blame arrived at via sloppy management or investigation. These are the smoking gun distractions – the obvious choice. But blame prefers the company of people, not systems, I.T. infrastructure, decisions, or machines. Someone designed, installed, and then maintained these things. Somebody made the relevant decisions. With the fullness of time, our gregarious little friend will find its own way home: back to the *actual* source – a human! And the source, more often than not, is to be found lurking within the management ranks.

When I demonstrated in previous jobs that I was a good worker yet was never promoted, I naturally blamed the managers. But how long could I go on blaming them – right up to my retirement? Would I spend the next thirty years blaming others for holding me back (Remember Jon's story in Chapter 1)? Maybe, but I would have been wrong to do so. I *knew* they were holding me back. I *knew* they would not change. Before long, the blame would migrate to me since I was the only factor in the equation that was capable of changing the result: I had to leave and move on. This is why in Chapter 1 we talked about taking responsibility for the here-and-now and the future, dropping blame and taking action.

This is of crucial importance in organizations. Blaming employees for making mistakes that go undetected or uncorrected for a period of time, or for which they are not properly trained, allows the blame to migrate to their manager.

Managers must have the courage to address the problem in an effective and meaningful way. We see a wide range of problems almost everyday in the work setting. People arriving late, not pulling their own weight, causing problems, spreading gossip, bullying and harassing, all done while the rest of us sit back and point the finger of blame at the offenders. In reality, however, the blame in such instances migrates very quickly from the actors to the audience.

Keep the Home Fires Burning

This concept is also important to you in your personal life. Standing on the sideline screaming injustice is a trick you can only perform for so long. While people will feel justified in blaming others for their problems for the rest of their lives *you* should avoid it. That kind of behavior only increases stress and causes cancer. Get out, walk away, cut your losses. It's only a job. You'll meet someone better.

A friend told me he woke up one day and both he and his wife realized they no longer knew each other. They both had very successful careers that involved long hours, travel - all the usual trappings. By all modern measures they were successful. But the marriage was doomed when reality came home to roost.

We have already looked at the idea of formulating a Life Plan for ourselves. In relation to your personal and family life, you should be asking yourself the following questions:

- Do I see my partner often enough?
- Is the time we spend together quality time?
- How well do I know my own children?
- What does my partner consider important in life?
- What do my kids consider important in life?
- Anything just happened, or in the calendar, that is important to them?

When we consider that divorce is becoming the *one in every two marriages* phenomenon,[78] questions such as these should be obvious. Remember, so much of the quality of our lives both at work and at home depends upon the quality of the questions we ask. Not asking them and not knowing the answers - and more importantly, not acting upon the answers – will in time see blame migrate to you when your marriage or family becomes a member of the unfortunate statistics group. Be aware of the reality of promise breaking. As busy people, we have a tendency to keep our promises with the world but break them with the family. The simple truth is this: family is easier to renege on. If we don't keep our promises with our children, for example, then we run the danger of receiving from them the same respect they receive from us. Stating later that we were simply too busy in the work aspect of our lives will be cold comfort indeed.

As an aside, I spend a lot of time telling people that management also involves the ability to shout Stop. Escalation – increasing commitment and spending on projects that really need to be killed off – is a growing problem in the business world. Sometimes you just have to pull the plug. It can be the same in personal issues. Never give up easily, but at the same time be aware of what Professor Joe McDonagh from Trinity College, Dublin, refers to as "Trying to cure an alcoholic by giving him one more drink". Indulging in escalation will see blame attach itself to you eventually.

---

[78] 50% is a predicted figure for the future with this predicted figure changing periodically from 50% to 43% to 40% and back to 50% again. See:
http://www.divorcereform.org/rates.html

Cover All the Angles

Family life and relationships are not just the only areas we should be guarding. Remember your Life Plan has key elements, each of which deserves attention. I, for example, was never brilliant with numbers. I have come to believe quite strongly over the years that it was not the numbers subjects but the way in which they were taught that was the problem. But the longer I use this as my source of comfort, the greater the likelihood that blame for my inability to properly invest for my own future and retirement will migrate away from all the school teachers and college professors to me.

The same can be said of my health. If I drink too much coffee, don't exercise, eat the wrong foods and work crazy hours, my health will go down the tubes fast. There's no point in me blaming coffee, bagels, my job, whatever, when later I'm hooked up to tubes when I should be out enjoying my retirement years. The blame must migrate to me. None of us have as much time in any day as we would like and yet when told we have cancer or a close loved one dies, perspective returns to show us what is truly important. As with the idea of a life plan, don't wait for tragedy, illness, or disaster to strike. Be proactive. Life's hard enough. Give yourself a fighting chance.

A Lot of Reasons are Excuses in Disguise

A manager told me of his disgust at not having been rewarded in terms of salary review. I decided to push him so as to gain an insight into his personality, his outlook for the future and his approach to solving what he perceived as problems within the department. I then explained to him that in reality he had three options:

- Shut-up and put-up;
- Change it;

> Leave.

He accepted that he could not change the way in which the company operated. He said he could not leave since he had children to think about so he was aware his only option was to stay quiet and put up with it all. I found this to be a very tragic conclusion on his part, and a worrying mindset for the department as a whole. It has been my experience that there is a world of difference between a reason and an excuse. Staying in a job you hate for your entire working life simply because you have a family is one of the most appalling *excuses* imaginable, and it is more common than you would think.

> If you find you dislike what you are doing, then sell up and change your life. Self-imposed misery is a kind of madness. The cure is to get out.[79]

This is something we have to watch out for in ourselves and in others. It is amazing how reasons, when examined closely, can actually turn out to be nothing more than excuses, and pathetic ones at that. Here we had a manager staying in a job where his employers clearly did not appreciate him, but he would stay there until retirement because he had children! There's something not quite right about that line of thinking. He seems to be begging blame to migrate to him in the future. Time and time again I have listened to arguments of this kind from managers. Take a look at the following excellent analogy:

> The syndrome of employment as ghost-marriage is a great danger to one's personal Voodoo. For better or for worse, for richer or poorer, staff stay on and on, not daring to imagine, let alone attempt, the single life again. This slow paralyzing of thought, innovation and empowerment

---

[79] Dennis (2007) p. 239.

wreaks havoc in time on any healthy organizational system – and on the personal system.[80]

Perhaps that manager – and people like him - is not fully to blame. You would expect that anyone appointing a manager would ensure they can manage, would get a feel for the type of person they are. And yet, the problem pops-up over and over again.

This particular manager has taught us about blame migrating, about the danger of reasons being excuses, and finally about complaining. Had he drawn up a life plan, managed his finances, kept 6-12 months salary in an easy to draw down account, he would not have felt trapped. The longer he stayed, the greater the likelihood of blame migrating. In the words of John F. McCormack, my late father:

> "If you ignore advice and refuse to act upon alternatives you give-up the right to complain".

Destroying the Last Refuge of the Coward

The existence of the *All Blame Migrates* principle must never be allowed equate to a call to cowardice. Far too many people, in an effort to avoid blame, will see doing nothing as the solution. We must therefore recognize another kind of blame.

What I term *Productive Blame*, is positive. It generates buy-in, strengthens commitment and builds trust. It occurs when an employee has tried to do something for the better, has tried to improve. They must take accountability for failing but it's a better class of failure because their intentions were precisely what you were looking for. You too will fail along the way. You'll fail to set suitable examples, you'll misread the context, you'll fail to constantly reassess – especially in the beginning. Trying something

---

[80] Carayol and Firth (2001) Pg. 177

new and better but failing does not see you attract negative and unproductive blame. Instead, you attract positive productive blame. A type of blame that reaches out with a helping hand to raise you back to your feet, says "Well done, good try, now go again". So long as recklessness and crass stupidity are absent, anyone trying to make things better (especially those who try to improve themselves as people and as managers) should always attract *productive* blame and not therefore worry about that particular class of blame migrating to them. In short, it is the migration of blame based on inaction, laziness, lack of consideration, doing the same old thing, etc, that we should worry about.

Some Final Thoughts

So we've spent some time looking at the idea that All Blame Migrates back to its original source. We recognize the Smoking Gun Syndrome that causes us to attach blame to the wrong places. We know that blame prefers people. If we accept these things, then we are demonstrating to ourselves that we have started to take on an internal locus of control approach to our lives. We have started dealing with short-term problems but with a long-term focus. This is exactly where we *should* be. Oh, it's not pretty and it takes a lot more bother and effort than settling for smoking guns. There is absolutely no guarantee you will not come across uncomfortable findings when seeking the true source of blame but in the long run we benefit ourselves, our families, our finances, our health, and all of those around us at work every day.[81] Isn't it worth going the extra mile for?

---

[81] Be mindful that when we speak of Blame Migrating we are speaking in a preventative and upfront sense. An organization run along the lines of attributing blame rather than learning from mistakes and working toward solutions is *not* what we are looking for here.

If we do not accept this principle, then we open the door to another: the Peter Principle – each of us rise to the level of our own incompetence. Why would we do this to ourselves? Why accept poor investigations that place blame on a secondary source – thereby placing ourselves in the league of incompetents? Time, effort, and discomfort, seem to be such fertile breeding grounds for short-term solutions with short-term focus. And yet, every day, it is these very excuses, masked as reasons, that managers opt for.

Chapter 4
Positive Consistency

At this point we really should be up and running. We have reassessed in light of knowledge concerning life's common pitfalls and the things that have been found to cause managers to derail. From here on out, we will constantly reassess our attitudes, perspectives, beliefs, assumptions, and more. We will learn to spot mistakes in others. We will start to unearth what is really going on behind what others show and tell us. This new ability instills in us a responsibility: if we ignore what comes to us via our newly developed abilities then we allow blame to migrate to us. Ignorance truly is bliss, but not for the person who has learned to analyze themselves, to reflect upon such analysis, to learn, and to manage themselves first, and then benefited from this when dealing with others. Simply put: an effective manager discovers more true causes via human interaction than the common manager. While appearing great on the surface, the ability to truly manage carries a heavier responsibility.

As we will see in this chapter, if we are inconsistent others will not trust us and thereby become difficult to manage. In other words, inconsistency springs from an inability to manage ourselves. And if we can't manage ourselves…

Positive and Negative Consistency

I will use these terms to differentiate between the various situations we encounter in both our personal and work lives. Consistently doing the wrong things, behaving in the wrong way, is Negative Consistency. The opposite, Positive Consistency, should therefore be obvious.[82] So we have inconsistency, and then consistency broken into two parts: negative and positive. The trick now is to stay alert and define each activity, behavior, system, methodology, perception, that you come across as either lacking in consistency, or as Positive or Negative Consistency. Doing so enables you to determine which stays and which ought to be reconfigured. This also helps put an end to any argument suggesting that in a world now governed by change consistency is out of place. Only the Negative Consistency aspects are out of place.

Watch the Outer Rings

In the grand scheme of things Positive Consistency is not that difficult. An organization should have a vision. A person should have a life plan. These act as your points of reference for everything else. I like to think of the vision for a company as the center point with larger and larger circles surrounding it. Each of these circles represents objectives, goals, etc. The Vision only requires reassessment at intervals; say once per year, depending on the industry and condition of the business.

Your personal life is the same. At the heart of things should be your Life Plan. This is something that can stay static for long periods of time. As you develop a strategy to pursue each of its

---

[82] As we will see later, however, a seemingly positively consistent process or system can turn to negative consistency if the process is devoid of context sensitive and constantly reassess. See Chapter 7.

elements – health, career, finance, etc – you add circles around the Life Plan. The further out you go, the more you must Constantly Reassess. The center is solid. Each circle beyond that becomes less stable but contains small everyday items which, if left without constant reassessment – can have a damaging cumulative effect.

This makes sense for both the working and personal aspects of our lives. If I ask you to commit a fraud at work or take heroin at home, you can immediately see the problem. These two new requests that I have put to you rock the core of your beliefs – fraud will ruin your professional life and hardcore drugs will ruin your personal life. Each will cross over and affect the other and all aspects of your life plan will be hit hard in a very negative way. But if I move to the outer most circles and, for example, I buy you a doughnut every morning for our 10am cup of coffee, you might simply come to see this as a welcome new distraction from the daily grind. But think about it. I now have you on coffee and doughnuts five days per week. 10am might actually be your second or third cup of coffee that day. Can you see now how the outer rings contain individual unimportant daily behaviors which, when added together, have a nasty cumulative effect? This is why I say the outer rings – those furthest from your point of reference – require Constantly Reassess more than the inner rings. The inner rings vibrate very clearly when interfered with but not the outer ones.

Getting Inside Their Heads

As we saw in previous chapters, the starting point is with ourselves. When I start focusing on my own level and display of consistency, I start to notice it in others. It's just like someone telling you they never see black cars on the streets any more. After that, all you see are black cars! Watching for a lack of consistency in others can be important. One of the subtle lessons to take from studying employee motivation is that a problem can manifest itself in a bizarre way. A lot of complaints about money, for example, have nothing to do with money, whether the person complaining recognizes this or not.

People say things like, *"I hate this place. My job is crap. They better give me a good pay raise this year"*. If a person is unhappy in their job, paying them more money simply means they become a richer unhappy person. They are still unhappy. The demand for more money is the symptom but not the cause. This particular inconsistency causes companies so much time, effort, and expense every year. It is another example of the Smoking Gun: a sloppy investigation reveals the person wants more money so we up their salary to stop them complaining, i.e. the lack of money becomes the secondary target for blame. Within a short period of time, they're unhappy again, productivity starts to drop off, absenteeism and a whole host of other things surface. And where do you think blame will migrate to?

Blowing Hot and Cold

I once worked for a manager who made everyone feel uneasy. Some mornings he would saunter through the building whistling like the happiest person in the world (he never seemed to be whistling anything recognizable – it was just whistling for the heck of it). Other days, he would arrive late, storm through the building, and disappear into his office. You would be forgiven for concluding that bi-polar depression is now a prerequisite for entering the managerial ranks. Waiting to see if someone will arrive whistling or slamming doors is not the way to run a business. It was the lack of consistency in that particular manager's mood that knocked us all off keel. If he was always happy or always an ass we could have lived with that.[83] Robert Sutton makes an excellent observation on this point:

> Their poison quickly infects others; even worse, if you let them make hiring decisions, they will start cloning themselves. Once people believe that they can get away with treating others with contempt or, worse yet, believe they will be praised and rewarded for it, a reign of psychological terror can spread throughout your organization that is damn hard to stop.[84]

Swinging from one extreme to the other – whether because of depression, alcohol, drugs, family difficulties, whatever - without any apparent reason can do a lot of damage. People who are consistent in mood and personality add comfort and reassurance to their surroundings. Everyone knows what they are dealing with. Imagine all hell breaking loose, you all look to your leader for guidance, but he's running in circles trying to jump out the window to escape. It is particularly during crises that any lack of consistency can be very damaging. If you generally appear calm, knowledgeable, etc, then when disaster strikes, any radical change from that general appearance will cause alarm. You may certainly develop a sense of urgency, strength of opinion; but moving from calm and knowledgeable to panicked, ranting, raving, is too far a leap. It is generally during bad times that real managers are discovered and the phonies uncovered.

The Inner Group of LMX

In the study of Leadership there is a theory known as Leader-Member Exchange Theory (LMX).[85] I have always found this to be an excellent reflection of the reality on the ground. The theory

---

[83] Granted, people with mood swings generally display greater creativity. See Carr (2004).
[84] Sutton (2007) p. 159
[85] See Yukl (2006).

works on the assumption that a manager will have an "inner group" – a small gathering of close "pals" or colleagues. As members of the inner group, they can expect to receive more interesting assignments, greater access to information, and have a greater number of tasks delegated to them. The return for the manager seems good too: greater commitment, going the extra mile, higher loyalty, etc. But for me, that's where the good aspects stop.

The people within the inner group come to believe they are one of the manager's "pals" due to their competence – they see this as distinguishing them from those excluded. The rest of the employees – surprise, surprise – view things differently. They simply view membership of the inner group as favoritism, politics, ingratiation.

We can immediately see a number of examples of inconsistency: the manager treating employees as two groups, and those two groups viewing each other differently. In other words, three different opinions from three different viewpoints.

But it gets worse. The manager in LMX Theory also views group performance differently. He will attribute success to factors internal to the members of the inner group and failure as having been caused by something external to them. How bizarre is that? The opposite is the case for members of the outer group – the majority of employees. He will give them less support yet blame them for failures more than he will blame members of the inner group.

I somehow found myself to be a member of an unofficial inner group in one of my earlier jobs. The manager would ask my opinion, advice, show me personnel records, tell me confidential things about individual employees, ask me to help plan ways of monitoring and disciplining people who were higher up the food chain than I was, show me senior management plans, memos, etc. It was great. I could play Rasputin to the Czar or Bismarck to the Kaiser.

Let me be clear here. I am not advocating the abandonment of teams, working groups, anything like that. What I am pointing to is the dangers of a constant unofficial secretive little group that breeds distrust, has access to information and decision-making processes that it should not have, and that is not held accountable in any way for the information it passes and receives, the decisions it influences, and the damage it causes – *Negative* Consistency. The damage is to the organizational culture, the trust, the psychological contracts of each employee. The list goes on.

Positive Consistency is a principle we ignore at our peril. How on earth can having a secretive group of pals, who are answerable to no-one, and in whom you have confidence to the degree that you automatically explain away failure as having been caused by anything other than the members, be beneficial? How can a lack of consistency in mood, temperament, attitude, reaction, in day-to-day dealings, be beneficial? When it comes to being either incredibly happy or incredibly sad, being either incredibly calm or incredibly angry, I like to think of a temperature gauge, just like one you'd see on a boiler or a water heater. The needle should never fluctuate so wildly that it drops below the 40% level or breach the 60% level. There is still ample room for a change of mood given the arrival of success or disaster, but the change is not so much as to add to problems.

My After Lunch Incident

As I indicated earlier, it is the small, seemingly unimportant things that can have a negative cumulative effect. The new phenomenon of working life is the Bullying Claim. It is a monster that has arisen for one reason and one reason only: bad management. The aspect of managerial practice in question is the breaching of the consistency principle. People are bullied simply by virtue of the fact they are treated differently – inconsistently (unless of course everyone's being bullied: Negative Consistency).

I saw this first hand a number of years ago. I arrived back to work late from lunch and shared the elevator with a work colleague who was also late. When we emerged from the elevator car, as a joke, she held the door open for me. The two of us entered onto the floor whereupon the junior manager immediately singled me out for being late while my colleague stepped around us. The reasons (excuses) for singling me out are irrelevant here. The point is that there was a blatant and overt demonstration of inconsistency on the part of the junior manager.

The ripples this sent through the organization were staggering. I was negatively affected. My colleague saw what had happened. Others witnessed it too. I went straight up the chain-of-command demanding they cage this junior manager (thereby extending the ramifications to four of the Five Constituencies – external stakeholders escaped). I am a true believer in the "No Assholes" Rule (thank you Robert Sutton).[86] This in turn led to conflict resolution, numbers of senior managers becoming involved, and more.

But the real point to take from this story is the dangerous results that flow from inconsistency leading to bullying, or simply claims of bullying. There can be no doubt that however favorable the outcome of the investigation for that junior manager, no matter how amicably it was all eventually settled between us, mud sticks! A moment's breach of the consistency principle, a seemingly small and irrelevant thing, has the potential to dog his career with that company. And remember; all industries, when you've been around

---

[86] See: The No Asshole Rule– *Building a Civilized Workplace and Surviving One That Isn't*. Sutton (2007).

long enough, are really small industries: everyone knows or knows of everyone else!

The Dangerous Power of Perceptions

One of the weird things in life is that we can see ourselves in a way that can be totally inconsistent with how others see us. And we're usually not aware of such differences because it's just not something we talk about. This can have devastating consequences in the family setting. A father, for example, might see himself as strong, proud, a good mentor, whereas his children – if asked – might refer to him as bossy, domineering, and intimidating. Examples such as this are more common than we know or would care to admit. The perceptions we hold of ourselves, of our abilities, of others, of the situation, can be dangerous – to ourselves and to others. The perception that a threat exists can put us on the defensive. Our defensiveness can be perceived by others as a threat and so they too react. And all because there was a *perception* of something existing rather than a fact of it actually existing.

Perceptions underpin Equity Theory of motivation. In the work-setting people make comparisons between themselves and those around them. They will form a judgment about the effort they put in and the reward they get out. They will also look at others under the same criteria. But it's all based on perception. So, I might hear a rumor that you were hired to do the same job I do but you got more money. I might also form a perception that you don't work as hard as I do. Now I have two perceptions at work: you get more money and you do less. This may be totally inconsistent with the facts but this never stops workers from following the process through to its damaging and illogical conclusion. From these perceptions I start to feel aggrieved – there is inequity and it's working against me. As a result, I can work harder, work less, cause trouble, pick on you, call in the union – lots of things. And all because of my perception of the situation and not what I know for sure.

But it's not all negative. The perception of help, of support, of the other side starting to doubt itself, can spur us on to attempt and achieve things we might not ordinarily try or dare dream of achieving. For now, however, let us simply register the fact in our minds: perceptions can be dangerous. They can cause us to breach the positive consistency principle.

Delegation[87]

We touched upon the idea of portfolio and job rotation earlier. That might have been a suitable place to mention delegation but I have always felt that delegation can lead to huge inconsistencies so I will deal with it here. I have often heard people remark over the years that, "A *manager's job is to delegate*". What a dangerous statement!

Delegating can be a terrifying experience for any manager. Giving a person a task to do really means that if they fail it is *you* who carries the blame. Delegation requires trust, sharing power, taking risk, taking the blame, facing fear, and more. But you must get the mix right. A failure to delegate means you forego the opportunity to ditch some of the Demands made of you. When you fail to ditch Demands, you retain Constraints that bar your own progression, development, promotion. Delegation can be a fantastic time management technique too.

All of these things are so much easier when tackled from a position of being able to manage yourself before trying to manage others. When you have planned across numerous fronts, when you have positive consistentcy in attitude, perspective, behavior, when

---

[87] This is a topic that is dealt with in more detail in the second book in the series: The 'PEOPLE' Factor. Go to www.JustManageIt.guru for further details.

you constantly reassess on all pertinent fronts, then the idea of delegating becomes less daunting. Getting so much right personally gives you a greater ability to understand others.

One of the key mantras of managerial life comes into play when dealing with delegation: *hire people smarter than you are.*

> It's your call. Believe in your own bullshit and grow steadily poorer, or listen to the people you employ and get richer and richer. I tried it the first way in the early days. When that didn't work, I got sensible and started a policy of deliberately employing men and women who were smarter than I was – and listening to them. It works every time.[88]

As a manager your job, particularly the higher up the ladder you climb, is not to be an expert in every single thing: you are there to *manage* the experts. In fact, you will generally find the higher you go the less technical knowledge you require so expertise starts to fall off as a prerequisite. You may be good at numbers but will probably end up hiring an accountant or investment analyst. You may have been good at marketing in college but will hire a brand manager. From this we can see that you should delegate things that others can do better than you. Remember, the better your team performs the better you look. The West has been moving toward specialist for years oblivious to the fact that a specialist should not be allowed to manage specialists. The Generalist is a dying breed that really does require an urgent kiss of life before we all find ourselves in misguided and badly managed companies. Be Specialist in function (if you must) but be generalist on the human level. We will return to the topic of Delegation in the second book in this Just Manage It! series.[89]

---

[88] Dennis (2007) p. 320.
[89] The 'PEOPLE' Factor: *Leading and Managing the People Around You*: McCormack (2010).

Consistency is Here to Stay

There really is no escaping the Positive Consistency principle when seeking to be an effective manager. Whether it's the way you deal with people, your mood, your reactions to different situations - a lack of Positive Consistency will come back to haunt you.[90] But it's not just behavioral issues. Don't formulate teams but then continue rewarding people for their individual achievements. Don't preach about cross-selling of services but then focus on billing hours.

A lack of consistency, just like we saw in my story of the junior manager singling me out for being late, leads to a world of troubles. Remember, others are watching, listening, recounting the tales: bad news spreads out to all Five Constituencies. Exaggerations and assumptions can make things even worse. It is crucial when dealing with the idea of consistency that the opportunity to set suitable examples is seized upon. If you show others that Positive Consistency is the norm, then such examples will in time spread to others, especially if you are in a senior and visible position.

No matter what the excuse (notice I have not said "reason") when you breach the Positive Consistency principle, not only do you set an unsuitable example for others: you set down a homing beacon for blame to migrate back to you at some point in the future. Inconsistency at a high ranking level will see similar poor behavior later from the new would-be managers who are watching the examples set. It really is all you can expect. Such an outcome will see blame migrate from those new ineffective managers to you. We also see this with our children. Set them bad examples and you can only blame yourself for the results. On a more worrying level, research indicates that inconsistent parental responsiveness can lead to attachment anxiety and attachment avoidance issues in later

---

[90] As Myers (2008) Module 21, indicates: moods influence how we interpret the actions, words and behavior of others – passions exaggerate.

life. Earlier we saw the ease with which we renege on promises to family. In other words, we tend to be inconsistent or negatively consistent on the home front in a number of ways.

Some Final Thoughts

We know from our own lives of the importance of watching the outer rings. Over time, small inconsistencies, oversights and omissions can have a devastating cumulative effect. Consistency of behavior – Positive Consistency as opposed to Negative Consistency – is the antidote to so many of our recurring problems. In addition to making our own lives easier, it enables others to view us as people and managers who are reliable, stable, and worthy of trust. If you find yourself behaving contrary to the Positive Consistency principle it should be an immediate indicator to you that your internal Constantly Reassess function is not operating as well as it should be.

If you are afraid to delegate then the problem is with you. If delegation is uncomfortable then it's usually a sign you're on the right track. If others need training, greater authority, etc., give it to them. Fear, courage, trusting others, etc., are matters you have to address in yourself. If others are trained and ready but you still can't delegate, then you are definitely incapable of managing yourself. This is a topic I will return to later in the second book of the series: The 'PEOPLE' Factor. For now, however, its reference here in this book has served its purpose: not being able to delegate points to a worrying factor within your overall managerial abilities. The how, when, what, and to whom aspects of delegation – plus the Five-Rs of delegation - will be covered in The 'PEOPLE' Factor.

Finally, as we will come to see later, Positive Consistency involves Action that is regulated by Context Sensitive via a process of Constantly Reassess.

Chapter 5
Three Muddy Puddles

One important lesson you should take from our discussion is this: we need to question and discuss a lot of everyday topics to make sure we are led by truth and not conventional wisdom – we must Constantly Reassess. René Descartes devised four laws, three of which should be of interest to us here.[91] First, don't accept something as true or certain unless you know for sure that it is true or certain – Constantly Reassess in our language. Second, break each problem down into as many parts as possible – BabySteps in our language. And third, start with the simplest parts and work your way up through the increasing layers of difficulty – focus and problem-solving in our language. As Descartes points out of this method, and something we should take comfort in:

> But the chief ground of my satisfaction with this method, was the assurance I had of thereby exercising my reason in all matters, if not with absolute perfection, at least with the greatest attainable by me...[92]

This chapter deals with three unpopular workplace issues, or muddy puddles: Ego, Politics, and Conflict. Simply mentioning them can conjure up unpleasant thoughts and connotations. But we

---
[91] Descartes (1637, 2004).
[92] Descartes (1637, 2004) Part II, p. 19.

must be careful here. Conventional "wisdom" will tell us we need to rid the workplace of these issues. These things – so goes the mantra – have no place in effective, efficient, and profitable companies. Remember; questions answered, answers questioned.[93]

Let us now return to the Hidden Self diagram that appeared earlier in the Introduction:[94]

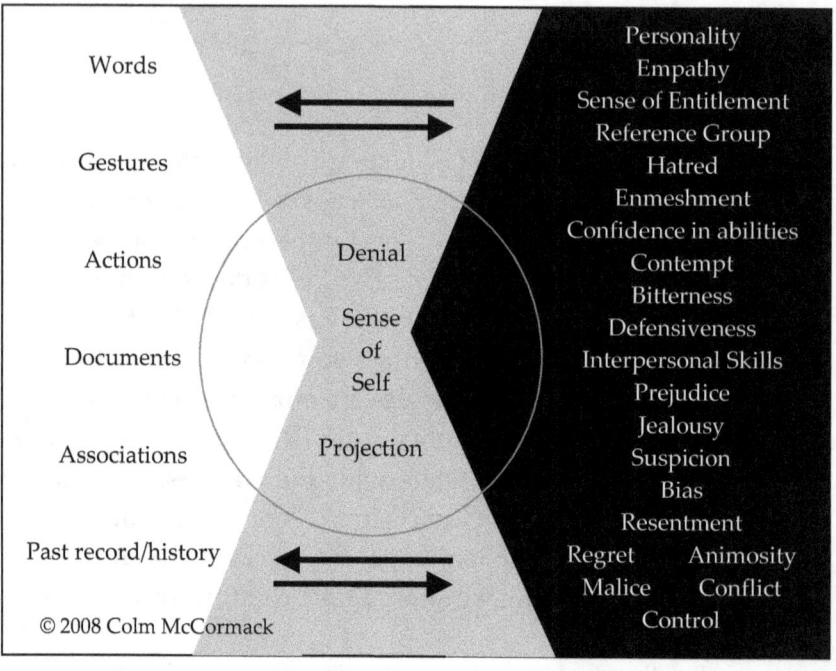

Ego, politics, and conflict – the subject matter of this present chapter – will all find foundation in the right-hand side of the Hidden Self diagram: it is the items on that side that motivate people to engage to differing degrees in politics, conflict and the

---

[93] Slogan of the Irish newspaper referred to earlier. See www.tribune.ie
[94] Again, as mentioned earlier, the list of items within this diagram is not intended to be exhaustive.

extent of control they exercise over their ego. But remember, you must discover these things in yourself first if you are ever to manage yourself effectively and recognize them in others. If you are in Denial over such issues lying in the shadows on the right-hand side of the diagram, then your Sense of Self may not be quite what it should and you may very well Project unnecessary things onto those around you by way of what you do, say, and produce.

1) Ego

Lots of people will rant about ego having no place at work, how it causes more harm than good. How many times have we been told to "leave your ego at the door"? But they miss the point entirely. And the truth is scary because it's not about killing ego: it's about *strengthening* it! 'Ego Strength' refers to our ability (or lack thereof) to maintain emotional stability and cope with stress. Yet, when referring to a person's ego getting in the way we are discussing a persons pride and their need to save face and protect reputation. Underlying such behavior is the presence or lack of ego strength. And that's what we should be considering: the underlying level of ego strength, building it, and using it. It's not about leaving your ego at the door. It's about refusing to proceed beyond the door without sufficient ego-strength.[95]

When it comes to managing others we can say that in the long run hurting others simply sees us hurting ourselves. Low self-esteem, self-worth and confidence, episodes of depression, addiction, boasting, defensiveness – these are just some of the signs of low ego-strength. And we can easily spot such behaviors within ourselves if we are honest and take time to reflect upon our behavior each day.

---

[95] See Hall, Michael L: www.neurosemantics.com/stuttering/egostrength.htm

Up to this point I have conveniently consigned one-to-one and group counseling sessions for managers to a footnote. But I make no secret of my views: colleges must amalgamate their business and psychology faculties, incorporate mandatory one-to-one and group counseling for all would-be managers. Sitting with psychology students, role playing, observing active listening in progress through the one-way windows of observational training rooms, takes management students away from the sole focus on business functions and closer to the human factors.

Building your ego strength can be done by following most of the items we discussed in Chapter one. Moving toward an internal locus of control, becoming more proactive and flexible in your thinking and actions, opening yourself up to change and leaning away from pessimism toward optimism all aid here. Remember what we said in chapter one. The common pitfalls in life are external locus of control, reacting, rigidity, negativity, resistance to change, etc, - all signs of low ego strength. And hopefully by now you've spotted the advantages of moving away from these. If you've been watching others you'll see how a failure on their part to move away from such attitudes and behaviors keeps them trapped in lives that change little for the better and casts them as poor choices for promotion to managerial positions.

You must take time to reflect upon your own behavior thereby learning about yourself. This is important because ego-defense mechanisms are unconscious – you will be unaware you are using them until they are pointed out to you, until you see the behavior in others, or until you analyze past situations and your own behavior. Many of Freud's[96] *defense mechanisms*[97] still make a lot of sense:

---

[96] I am not a fan of the Freud approach of focusing on the past, surfacing unpleasant past experiences, etc. It runs totally against my own personal philosophy of dealing with today, moving forward. Although I must readily accept the existence of research indicating that dwelling upon issues can sometimes be beneficial.

[97] Mullins, (2005).

Regression	Simply refers to behaving like a child. We have all seen temper tantrums, door slamming and shouting by managers. As managers we should expect ourselves to be much better than this. You cannot always get your own way *even* when *you're* the boss!
Rationalization	Refers to covering your own ass when things are seen to go wrong. Just as it takes a grown-up to accept he cannot always get his way, it takes courage to admit when we are wrong, when we said something we shouldn't have, or when it was us who suggested a plan that eventually led to losses. Mark H. McCormack touches upon this point in a very interesting way when he highlights three phrases managers find difficult to say: *I don't know, I need help, I was wrong.*[98] You rarely hear managers saying these things.[99]
Projection	Refers to people projecting feelings and motives onto others in order to protect their own egos. This is simply passing the book. As a manager, you are expected to have emotional maturity and emotional intelligence.
Fixation	Should be the one to guard against most. After all, you should be where you are because you don't throw childish tantrums, you are not afraid to admit a weakness and you take accountability for your actions. Inflexibility of attitude and approach should be the only thing to guard against. And yet it is the easiest to fall foul of.

You will see that I have broken the four defense mechanisms into three and one. Three are fundamental basics for being a mature human being. In fact, strong commitment is usually demanded of a manager in the job description. Here, however, we are seeing a link between your ego and the need to *Constantly Reassess*. You should

---

[98] McCormack (1984).

[99] Thankfully, however, the age of thinking that admitting a weakness actually makes you look weak is passing. In fact, it has often been found that people are drawn to leaders who confess to having a weakness, having made a mistake, or not having known all the answers.

always be looking at your own attitude, your criteria and your level of commitment. Are they all suitable? Has anything changed to render your approach out of place?

Of course, Freud discussed more than just four defense mechanisms but detailing them all might simply kill off any attention span a business person has for this kind of thing. There is, however, a fifth mechanism worth mentioning as it can dilute the harmful effects of *Fixation*. This mechanism is referred to as *Intellectualization*.[100] Intellectualization allows us to confront hurtful topics by removing the emotional aspect. We do this by looking at a situation in a logical and detached way, much as we did when using the Five Constituency model. This is very useful in organizations. There are plenty of examples out there of failed projects and millions of dollars poured into keeping them alive in the hope they will eventually come good. Standing back and looking at them in an objective and emotionally detached way would enable us to spot when we are on the wrong track and when *fixation* has kicked in.

> If you suspect you are leading the company headlong down the wrong path, there is more shame in not saying anything than in deciding to pull the plug…there are times when you simply have to cut your losses.[101]

So what we have now, without becoming overly indulged in the world of head-doctors, is a three-two split to keep in mind when viewing how we defend our egos. Three childish mechanisms, one adult mechanism, and one mechanism that serves as a remedy to the others.

The development of ego-strength is essential for any would-be manager. You have to allow for the possibility of including yourself as part of any performance problem your subordinates have and

---

[100] Hergenhahn et al (2003).
[101] Robinson (2004) pg 116.

therefore have to be able to include your own actions and behaviors as part of the solution. Allowing an underperforming subordinate comment on your behavior when discussing the problem is essential (constantly reassess) and takes good ego-strength.

2) Politics

Politics is a deeply human interactive process. In so many ways, being a manager casts you as a politician: meetings, memos, letters, reports – wording them, timing them, withholding them.

The mere mention of politics generally conjures up negative connotations and dark personalities. And we have all seen the signs: closed doors and blinds, whispers in the corridors, scheming in bars after hours, ingratiation and doing favors, forming coalitions, impression and information management, excluding people from meetings...the list goes on. A politically charged organization can suffer a number of debilitating symptoms: mistrust, reduced job satisfaction, reduced performance, lost time, poor information sharing, high communication barriers, high levels of anxiety and stress, and more.

An alternative perspective is that political behavior within organizations can be positive and is necessary in bringing about change and agreed courses of action. The fact is, as a manager you cannot survive or hope to go far alone and unaided. Management is about leverage. Change is about getting people onboard, building a coalition of supporters, isolating and removing troublemakers. Everything you do as a manager is about people. The people are the tools you use. Simply because people do not openly agree to help a manager does not mean the manager gets things done alone.[102]

---

[102] You will recall my mentioning a difference between "control" and "influence" in chapter one.

Therefore, to stay out of politics is to deny yourself many of the vital tools necessary for managerial success.

It would be a mistake, however, to conclude that all organizations suffering from high levels of negative political behavior suffer in terms of profitability. I myself worked for a company crippled by organizational politics yet it doubled its assets from € 500m to over € 1bn in 6 years. Another thing we must guard against is rushing to shoot the guy we view as the source of all politics in an organization. A lawyer in Bahrain told me that his boss was always viewed as difficult and frustrating to deal with because he was so political. It was only when the boss moved to another firm that the lawyer realized just how much crap his boss had been protecting everyone from.

It is not enough to ask what you will do as a manager. The crucial question may very well be: *why* (politics) will you do what you do?[103] It is crucial that every manager have an external network of trusted advisors, people who can advise on political issues.[104] The higher you rise within an organization the more political things become. It's just one of those facts of organizational life. To get anything done, you need support.

And politics happens at home too.[105] Kids know which parent to approach depending upon the topic. Sometimes they will set parents against each other or against the other children in the house however sensible (or not) their reasons and aims might be. It is the existence of an aim or desired outcome that casts the behavior as political rather than simply manipulative. Often, a parent will use politics in the family setting to avoid trouble, to steer a troublesome

---

[103] Butcher et al (2003).
[104] See Watkins (2003) who advises that all executives should have an external network loyal to them *not* to their company thereby ensuring reliability, honesty and frankness.
[105] Granted, our definition of "politics" is swaying heavily in the breeze here! And perhaps that is a large part of the problem: differing definitions of politics – whether people recognize they are defining it differently from one another or not.

teenager, or to sidestep an interfering in-law. Sometimes we take family votes around the dinner table on issues. Knowing a family vote will arise can see kids actually dealing and bargaining with each other before hand. And perhaps parents too! Just because you don't call it politics doesn't mean it's not politics. And it can be a crucial activity at home. If we accept that, ignoring the importance and usefulness of politics in the workplace is hypocritical.

3) Conflict

You must recognize that if conflict is left unattended to, ignored, rationalized away, it becomes worse. It will continue to become worse until someone realizes it requires attention. You should start to view conflict as a welcome occurrence since it offers you an opportunity to surface differences and misunderstandings, to deal with them, to look at the people involved. If you and I hate each others guts but never deal with the issue, then it continues to escalate. We might start avoiding each other, spreading gossip, splitting other peoples' allegiances. But allowing the conflict to surface and then dealing with it in a constructive way allows us to restore or establish well-being. Therefore, conflict can be said to escalate until such time as well-being is achieved.[106]

Conflict itself is not so much the danger as the inability and unwillingness to recognize and deal with it. One of the great problems of management in today's world is that socio-emotional issues can turn out to be a manager's Achilles Heel.[107] Conflict management, confrontation, and effective listening are not high on the subject agendas of Business Schools.[108] Negative emotions in a

---

[106] Humphreys (2006).
[107] Roberto (2005).
[108] The reality is thatBusiness School teaches via a process of *delayed* reflection but only if the student chooses to reflect later upon the lessons taught. That reflection can occur at intervals over many years *post*-graduation. Therefore, simply scoring high is not enough. You have not

conflict very often shatter reason. They can instill in us a sense of tunnel vision. During conflict you stop listening. You also stop asking questions. You will become so focused on ramming your point down the other person's throat that you will see no need to ask questions. A difference of opinion is rarely the problem in conflict: it is the lack of skills to deal with such situations that can be the real culprit. If you are truly capable of managing yourself you will be able to confront people in a meaningful and healthy way for the benefit of all concerned.

Remember that it is vital to carry out up-front investigations before you jump in with both feet. Be consistent here. Always look into something first. Constantly Reassess what you're hearing, who you're hearing it from, any attribution errors you might make. This applies at home too. Positive Consistency is of the utmost importance. Investigate problems at home before diving in. Whether at home or at work, a culture that is comfortable with and that actively encourages healthy and meaningful confrontation and the resolution of conflict is what we are looking for. Clear the air at home. Clear it at work too. Make life easier for yourself and everyone around you. Those watching your suitable examples will start to follow your lead.

But you can never get this far if your so-called management training has been devoid of the key elements of observing, interacting, reflecting, learning, engendering trust, inviting input from all levels, effective listening, reassessing constantly, etc. None of the issues we have discussed in this chapter is a monster. It is our

---

been placed in scenario after scenario during college to instill in you an ability to effectively deal with what matters. Learning how to manage – in the current business schools setup – comes in the years *after* the exams not the years leading up to them. With a lot of students firing their notes into the garbage after college, what chance do they have? And if they've never been taught to reflect, to Constantly Reassess, then what might we hope for?

perspective - checked by context - that can make them useful, enabling, and cast them as developers rather than inhibitors.

Observing Both Sides from No-Mans Land

The next time an argument or heated debate erupts in work, observe what is transpiring with the following questions in mind:

- Does it seem skilled, prepared, constructive?
- Can you determine who has valid points? Might negative perceptions held by any of the parties be involved? Do you get a sense they investigated such perceptions before acting?
- Does any of the conflict seem worthwhile? How is it impacting upon the Five Constituencies?
- Do you think they'll benefit from this episode or might they be making matters worse?
- Are they getting personal?
- Has tunnel-vision set in?
- Has pride taken over? Are they listening? Are they asking questions?
- Can you determine whether or not either party has significant ego strength?
- Is there anything in their argument that might suggest politics is at work (of either the positive or negative variety)?
- With the results from your Five Constituencies analysis, what do you think could be done to resolve the conflict in a more meaningful and beneficial way to the benefit of all Five Constituencies (i.e. can you limit the fallout while at the same time retaining effectiveness)?

Some Final Thoughts

Never lose sight of what I refer to as the 'darker side' of leadership and management techniques; avoiding things such as organizational politics, for example, because of all the negative connotations associated with it does not mean you should indulge in complete ignorance of it since others may use such techniques – the 'darker side' – against you.

We see this with ego and manipulation; some people deliberately utter things knowing it will set someone else off to their detriment and/or to the benefit of the utterer.

Far too often – both in personal and in work life – we avoid confrontation and conflict. But we can never be effective as indiviudals or as teams if confrontation is absent. Each of us needs to be told when we are off course or presenting as an obstacle to others. Yes, hearing such things with others watching can be very uncomfortable – remember; you develop as a humanbeing *outside* your comfort zone! To this end, confrontation takes on a positive, a beneficial, and indeed an essential contribution for personal and organizational effectiveness.

The same can also be said of conflict. Remember; conflict will continue to escalate until such time as well-being is achieved or restored. When seeking to lead or manage others, you must never ignore conflict or allow it to fester – you do so to the detriment of those involved and ultimately cause untold damage to the organization as a whole. Ignoring it will, in time, see blame for the adverse consquences migrate to you.

Chapter 6
Communication

It is not so much the case that everything we have covered so far has led us to this point: everything has sprung from here. All we have covered up to now has been very heavily reliant upon communication.

> ...people are often comfortable with not communicating well. Why? Because it protects them from confronting problems head-on, and saves them from having to make difficult decisions...while they are fudging and bluffing and blustering, the wrong people are in the wrong jobs, tasks are being performed below standard, essential action points are not being followed up, opportunities are being lost and the business is going down the tubes.[109]

One of the things I don't like about a lot of business school subjects is the way in which communication is relegated to a position of subtlety. It is always there, lurking in the shadows, with some professors failing to bring it out into the light at all. But it shouldn't be in the shadows. It is absolutely crucial to everything we do in management.[110] Remember, organizations are simply collections of people all supposedly chasing the same organizational vision. Take, for example, the simple marketing mix

---

[109] Robinson (2004) p. 126-127.
[110] In fact, horrific child sex abuse very often continues for as long as it does due to poor communications within and between various agencies and bodies.

of product, price, place, and promotion. Absolutely everything about those four Ps is communication:

- What does the product say about you when others see you with it?
- What does the price say about the product?
- The locations this product or service is sold say something;
- As does the advertising, packaging, coloring.

It is all about communicating. Strategy cannot be executed other than through people. Here's one for you: What's the difference between a target, an aim, a goal, and an objective? A lot of executives express surprise when they hear my usual answer to this: who cares! Chances are the person sitting beside you will see things differently, won't use the same definitions. You could travel half way around the world to meet someone and not realize you are both talking at cross purposes. All of this can see you fighting with your own executives. Communication is such a crucial aspect of management. The last thing you want to do is deliberately or unwittingly scupper your own chances of success by not getting to grips with proper, effective, and suitable communication. Particularly when dealing with people, perceptions not surfaced, unspoken assumptions – all can render people unnecessary enemies for years, and in some cases, for a lifetime.

> The manager is well aware that staff morale is the life-blood of the organization and that open, congruent, authentic, direct and clear communication is the heart that pumps that life-blood.[111]

---

[111] Humphreys (2006) p. 63.

Dangerous Assumptions

Get the communication issues wrong and your managerial career is over! On the surface, it will appear that the problem is with everyone else, but release blame and watch to whom she migrates. It is absolutely crucial that communication is very high on the agenda of any manager. Our failure to remove barriers to effective communication is a real problem.

Studies have shown that managers can spend up to 80% of their day communicating. My own view is that the greater portion of the remaining 20% is spent dealing with the by-products of communication – reports, figures, problems – or getting ready to send or receive communications. One of the shocking aspects to come out of this is that a lot of people who spend years working together can often – without realizing it – be working under different assumptions. There is the very real possibility you are all actually pulling in different directions albeit to subtle degrees. This is a well recognized issue within management academia. A simple difference in assumptions can very often be the foundation for organizational conflict.[112] In truth, the lack of communication about assumptions leads to people fighting without them knowing why it is they are fighting against each other. Let me give you an example.

I encountered an incredible difference in assumptions at a large law firm. One of the partners told me that if the firm was confronted by two people of equal wealth, one in a jogging suit and the other in a bowler hat, they would pick the person in the bowler hat. When I relayed this to the managing partners there was a unanimous reaction of dismissal, of labeling the story as nonsense. Yet there it was: one of their own had a totally different assumption about the type of clients they would take on despite there being a so-called organization-wide understanding of the firm's strategy. And of course their reaction left a lot to be desired too. But we can

---

[112] I have already mentioned this in the previous chapter.

see how ineffective communication caused consequences to surface in the most bizarre way.

This Can't Go On Any Longer

In businesses all around the world functional silos very often mean that communications must keep going higher and higher up the chain until they encounter someone in common with the two silos that want to communicate with each other. It is just astonishing how few of us ever stop, stand still at work, and think about this absurdity. And you'll find a lot of prestigious business schools laboring under committees, policies, rules, nonsense, but then sending professors into the classroom to lecture about the need for effective communication. Business schools don't always practice what they preach!

This scenario of having to go vertically up the structure rather than directly to the person you want to communicate with becomes worse when gatekeepers stand between silos. Add the *communication goes up through filters but comes down through loudspeakers* reality that exists in so many organizations and you have a real nightmare.

So why on earth do people not only preside over such scenarios, but perpetuate them to their own detriment? A large part of the answer comes down to the irony of the business world being too busy to stop and implement solutions that will make it less busy.[113] The foundation of the answer, however, is to be found in the failure to Constantly Reassess. If communication in your organization is crap, and if you've always known it to be that way, then why perpetuate it? Since you are in the managerial ranks there is an onus upon you to do something about it. If you do nothing, then stop complaining about it otherwise blame will migrate to you.

---

[113] Davenport and Prusak (2002).

Doing nothing means you are enforcing constraints against yourself and this is akin to doing a large portion of your competitors' work for them. Your stupidity can actually constitute a competitive advantage to your competitors. So manage the communication – don't let *it* manage you!

Communication and the Five Constituencies

The simple truth is that your employees need honest feedback if they are ever to improve or feel valued. They constitute a huge expense for your organization so not listening to them, not talking with them, makes little sense. Of course, there is a delicate mix to be struck between honesty and encouragement particularly when people are not doing as well as you had hoped. It is crucial that feedback be viewed as an act of nurturance, and not a reprimanding or reprimand-avoiding exercise.[114] We sometimes forget that giving feedback can be uncomfortable for employees. It is vital that fear is not a factor within your organization. How can employees receive feedback effectively themselves if they are afraid to question or comment on it? The presence of fear and the absence of trust are key barriers we must be alert to. They can prevent feedback becoming the two-way process it should be. Not correcting such a situation means we create extra unnecessary work for ourselves by allowing such barriers to stand.[115]

---

[114] Humphreys (2006)

[115] And yet it is astonishing just how many managers view the consequences of these barriers - fire fighting, sending memo after memo, dealing with trade unions – as normal everyday parts of their jobs. Working hard dealing with symptoms instead of working smart by dealing with the cause doesn't make a lick of sense. Bear in mind the theory of Demands, Constraints, and Choices. Choose effective communication and you will free up a lot of Constraints and lessen the Demands made of you. Choose not to do this and to whom do you think blame will migrate for your job being the way it is?

At this point, we will move on from employees. Again, let us revisit the Five Constituencies:

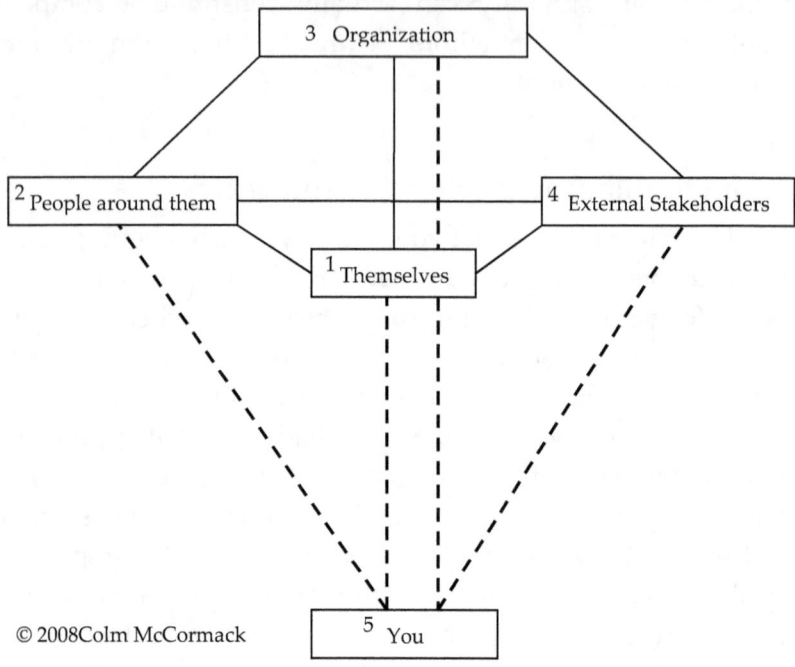

You, as manager, also require feedback. If you think general employees are expensive, you should take a look at your annual management salary figures. If employees should be developed to maximize your return on investment then so too should managers. As we have seen, we cannot rely on managers to activate their own Constantly Reassess function. Therefore, an absence of feedback – especially from those benefiting or suffering at their hand – is dangerous.

The third constituency in all of this is the organization or business itself. It cannot implement strategies other than through people. The big *'E'* – execution – was something that Jack Welch always harped on about.[116] Many strategies are executed incorrectly because they fall down on the people issues. And a lot of the people issues center around communication.

So, in terms of the five constituencies, employees need effective communication to know what they are doing, how they are doing, to give valuable input; managers require effective communication to learn about themselves, to manage employees; the organization requires effective communication to ensure that strategies are implemented through the people working within it; communication to and from external stakeholders is vital; the people around the person or team you give feedback to must also be kept in contemplation.

Stick a Sock in it!

It is so easy to forget that communicating involves listening. There is an old phrase that rings so true: *You have one mouth and two ears – use them in that proportion*!

One of the golden rules of business is, *listen to your customer*. Fail to do that and at some point you will find yourself customer-less, missing golden opportunities, failing to avoid deadly threats, and more. People signing up to your website should certainly be submitting useful information to you as they do so. But more importantly, you must be analysing and acting upon such information on a regular basis. Too many companies fail to systematically trawl the gold that is information coming to them – a failure to *listen*. It is akin to sitting in a room full of food yet stupidly dying of starvation.

Listening is one thing, but what I term *'Effective* Listening' is something better altogether. For me, the concept of effective

---

[116] Krames (2005).

listening is something that *must* be taught in all business schools. Why it is ignored is simply baffling.

Effective listening is a concept I like because I am a great believer in the *hearing but not listening* syndrome that afflicts so many managers when someone of lower rank is talking to them.

Some say 'Active Listening,' others will tell you 'Empathetic Listening' – the key point, however, should be this: find out what the person is saying, what they actually mean, how they really feel about the issue and what this all comes down to in their world. Only by understanding from their perspective can you see how to communicate back to them in a truly effective way.

Effective listening, therefore, is more than mere listening. It involves deeper understanding and response to the feelings that lie behind the words. For example, when a student would come to me and tell me they could not do a project I didn't automatically reply, "Yes you can". Instead, I had to reach in behind the words to see what feelings were underpinning them. Perhaps the student had low self-confidence, perhaps that was the first time they had ever carried out a project, perhaps – because I insisted on teaching experienced workers and executives and not students fresh out of high school – this person was coming back to school after many years not school- or exam-fit, perhaps they didn't fully grasp what was being said in the lectures or the project handbook.

Remember; emotions felt are not always emotions expressed! So, if instead of, "Yes you can", I simply asked, "Why, what makes you think that?" then I could start to unearth what was really going on. I would also reflect back to the person the feelings I thought I was picking up on just to be sure I heard it right and to make sure the person actually said what they meant. For example, they might say, "I'm worried I won't do this properly or it won't be good enough", to which I might reply, "So what you are saying to me is that you feel…"[117] In addition to listening to the words I will be watching the silent cues: facial expressions, posture, body language.

Don't listen simply to confirm your own views or to gather evidence to dismiss them. Make sure you silence the internal monologue running through your own brain – manage yourself! Don't blindly mimic their words back to them as some active listening techniques might cause you to do. A parrot can mimic but has no idea what it is saying – so, don't be a parrot! Instead, rephrase it to them to see if they agree you heard them correctly. Don't just juggle the words around: rephrase the feelings and emotions to get at what is really going on.

> [Effective] listening improves not only what you hear, but also what they say.[118]

So, I am *managing* the communication exchange between us. Oh yes, it takes a little longer and a greater degree of effort. But simply view it as front-loading the effort. Doing things the other way, i.e. not listening properly, can simply see you spending your working days trying to fix things because everyone is at cross purposes, unhappy. Listen upfront and you won't have to fire-fight later.

Try this at home. It will benefit your family and children. It's a very good practice to get into and will create a happier environment by diffusing arguments before they get out of hand (especially if there's a teenager in the house). Practicing these principles at home allows your kids to go out into the world better prepared for life and all the potential positive interactions with others this can bring. Good listening will deliver, at a minimum,

---

[117] Reflecting communicates empathy, understanding and validation.
[118] Fisher et al. (1981) p.35 – square brackets added with 'effective' inserted in place of the more common 'active'.

four positive outcomes: information, understanding, listening in return, and cooperation.[119]

But know this: effective listening can be incredibly tiring at first. I have heard new counseling psychologists complain about this during their training. Listening properly can wear you down and you need to build up your stamina. Just like the Fat Friday concept, don't be too worried about the occasional relapse at the start. These will occur until you become what I refer to as "listening fit". And remember, it can be tough when you've landed in a new managerial job with all those new faces with their ready-made problems, long-held grudges, etc. So structure your days to fit your listening fitness. Manage the stampede to your door. Once you settle in, then the flood to the "new manager's door" should slow to a trickle. At that point you are in a position to use effective listening in everything you do simply because your days become filled with small items rather than big intricate personnel issues. You may also find that listening becomes contagious. People react in kind and listen in return if they feel you are listening to them - all taking you closer to and enhancing the human interaction dynamics that are leading and managing.

A Picture Still Says a Thousand Words

When you shut-up, you can listen, you can effectively listen, but you can also observe too. This is important. Studies have found that up to 55% of a person's reaction to another's communication is due to facial expressions.[120] Think about what that is saying. The words from the person talking are not as important as you might otherwise think. It is their facial expressions that have a greater

---

[119] Stanton (2004)
[120] Vecchio (2006) quoting Mehrabian and Wiener.

effect upon how you react to them.[121] Now we are starting to see that communicating is not just about talking or sending memos or emails. It's also about observation, about non-verbal communication - gestures, expressions, posture, appearance – this is why I told you earlier to spend time observing others without interfering. Employees learn more from their eyes than from their ears.[122] You will remember my reference to watching a student's body language and facial expressions when discussing a problem and using effective listening. Has a friend ever told you their job interview didn't go well? They can often come to this conclusion via communication interpretive skills they're not even aware of. When on edge or cornered, these skills come into use but our lack of knowledge about them usually sees us labeling our insights as "intuition".

Studies over the years have shown, for example, that teachers, doctors, and judges can affect how students, patients and jurors behave via unwitting communication signals and cues. Numerous laboratory studies have also come into doubt since experimenters' expectations can often be communicated subtly and unwittingly to the subjects taking part in the tests.[123] In other words, communication comes in many forms, including the unintended variety.

Firing someone communicates a message. Bringing outsiders into the company communicates a very clear message about change. Setting suitable examples communicates to people. So things you do, actions you take, all of these things are incredibly important communications to anyone within the Five Constituencies who may be watching from a distance. Such

---

[121] The meaning of facial expressions have also been found to be culturally determined. See Averill, (1997) *The Emotions: an integrative approach*. In Carr (2004).
[122] Adair (1983).
[123] Rosenthal, Robert: *Covert Communication in Laboratories, Classrooms, and the Truly Real World*. Current Directions in Psychological Science, 12, 2003, 151-154.

techniques are used deliberately in change management: building guiding teams, coalitions, isolating trouble-makers, bringing supporters onboard, removing key executives and replacing them with your own change experts - all of these contribute to communicating that the change is going ahead and resistance will be dealt with. Words, pictures, sounds, doing things, not doing things[124] – they all communicate.

Lighten Up a Little

There is generally an error among managers of considering communication to be a formal and official animal. This is a damaging perspective to adopt. Take as an example IBM's reaction to people gathering at the water cooler when the company found itself in difficulties. The then chairman sent a memo telling people to get back to work. In reality, however, they were chatting with each other informally to find ways out of the difficulties.[125] Japanese companies use chat rooms where employees can spend twenty minutes or so chatting with each other about their projects. Irish companies often use social occasions to strike deals, obtain information, recruit, etc. All of these things require communication and all of it is largely informal. In fact, one professor at Trinity College, Dublin, regularly tells his MBA students that the best way to discover the type of organizational culture, the troublesome stakeholders, and the political stumbling blocks of an organization is to get away from the formal setting and take people out for a few beers.

We also know from our own working experiences that a lot of things get sorted out by passing people in corridors, on the back stairs, in elevators, and in bathrooms. Look at all the deals struck on

---

[124] Not doing anything often sends a louder message than doing something – a point very often lost on ineffective or cowardly managers.
[125] Davenport and Prusak (1998, 2000)

the golf course.[126] The informality of it all, and the absence of the crowd, can make such encounters communication goldmines.

What's the Return on Investment for Your Communication Effort?

Without indulging in micromanaging, it is crucial to test whether or not your communication was received and understood. This becomes particularly important when it comes to strategy. Fighting through the dead zone and using your last ounce of energy to reach the summit of Mount Everest does not mean you have made it: the summit is only the half-way point – you have to fight all the way back down too! Likewise, telling people what the new strategy is and how it works is only half the battle. You then need to test them on it to make sure that what you said was what they heard. Some companies have become incredibly clever on this aspect. Motorola, for example, has used interactive communications whereby employees get information from the company intranet but also have to answer quick-fire multiple-choice questions and surveys to test the level of their understanding and to obtain their views on important organizational initiatives.[127]

I like the idea of always testing the success of communications. Since as a manager you will spend 80% or more of your day involved in various communications, it would be nice to know whether or not this is time well spent. But particularly in relation to the crucial matters: strategy, product launches, learning programs. While it is important to consider employees as intelligent and capable people, it is silly to assume that just because *you* understand the message you are communicating, it will be

---

[126] Important deals struck on the golf course is a statement attributed to Donald Trump. See his book: The Art of the Comeback.
[127] Kaplan & Norton (2001)

interpreted in the way in which you intend it to be. This requires a change of perspective – to Constantly Reassess. By checking to see that your communication on important things was interpreted and understood correctly, you are also making *employees'* lives easier, not just your own. The organization also benefits from this quick and easy testing.

And that's the point. Good management should be easy: simplicity and genius often walk hand-in-hand. The amount of time it takes to check out the effect of a communication pales in comparison to the time it takes to correct strategic drift that can arise if no check is ever carried out.

Breaking Down the Walls

Professor Kingston from Trinity College, Dublin, warns against compounding intellectual differences by erecting physical barriers.[128] This is something I agree with strongly. Separate canteens, restrooms, chat rooms, etc, are just not the way to go. If they exist, tear them down. Plop everyone into common areas. Peters and Waterman, in their *In Search of Excellence*,[129] indicate that excellent companies maintain high intensity communication and focus on informality. The reality of organizational life usually means functional departments. From this has come the idea that strategy, project management, training, change, and now communication, must be cross-functional in order to be truly effective. So how is this to be achieved?

You should refuse to manage without walking around. Why remain in your office away from the people who know the company best: the workers. There will be an instant backlash from some quarters to this suggestion on the grounds of time and

---

[128] Kingston (2003).
[129] Peters, Thomas J., and Waterman Jr., Robert, H. (1982).

advances in technology. But if we go back to the idea of facial expressions constituting a vital component of communication, then the idea of managing by walking around retains its importance. If you don't have enough time then you are managing the wrong things. How can you not have enough time to make sure the building is running properly, that people are not killing each other, that you are not missing vital suggestions, input and solutions from workers? Carlos Ghosn, CEO of Renault Nissan, is famous for walking around the factory floors and intermingling with the workers. J.W. Marriott Jr. logs over 160,000 air miles per year visiting his company's hotels.[130] The founder of Ikea continues to visit stores to stay in touch.[131] So if the guys handling billions of dollars every year can do it, what's *your* problem?

But remember that management by walking around is not about walking around. I have watched executives make this mistake countless times. They operate on the idea of striking fear into the workers: fear of being caught slacking, using the internet, chatting on the telephone, whatever. That is not management: it's manipulation, it's prison camp guard behavior. Management by walking around infers the ability to approach, communicate with and effectively listen to workers. In the 1980s, the conventional wisdom was to keep in close contact with managers two layers beneath you in the hierarchy to make sure you were hearing what was actually going on.[132] But this is not enough. If a manager can't chat with the people who stock the canteen, sweep the floors, take out the trash, input the data…with anybody at any level, then they do not deserve to be a manager. Remember, management is a human experience – an activity. Not doing these things sets unsuitable examples for others. It foregoes placing yourself in situations to hear things that may set off your internal Constantly

---

[130] Dessler (2004)
[131] Jennings (2002)
[132] See: McCormack (1984).

Reassess alarm. If something bad occurs later, and people at the bottom could see it coming, then blame will migrate to the manager who refused to manage by walking around.

But How Do I Get Started?

This is a very common question. Some managers have never managed by walking around before or they've been locked away in their offices for years and don't know how to get started without raising suspicion in the minds of their employees.

One of the first things I tell managers to do is up the friendliness factor. Take the simple step of saying Hi whenever you pass employees. Don't bury your head in a file or start reading when you see them coming toward you in the corridor. And say hi outside of work too. You might see them in the parking lot, in the Mall – wherever – just say hi and acknowledge their existence. At work, if they don't see you simply say out loud, "Good morning everyone". That's all: nothing fancy. You're simply breaking the ice and getting them use to the idea you want to interact with them.

Second, be patient. It takes time to generate trust and to put yourself across as being trustworthy.

Third, be genuine. Why are you doing this - simply to get info to hang them with? Be careful here: there's a world of difference between manipulation and motivation. Employees will instantly spot you as a fraud if you are on the manipulation track. You *should* be doing this to ensure that what you hear from your direct reports is the actual truth, to show employees that they can offer feedback to you directly, and more.

Fourth, ask everyday-type questions. Information will come to you over time. Don't rush it. If you hear a worker has a child who is sick, for example, or plays for a soccer team, ask a polite question about that. Be friendly, be genuine, and after a period of time people will start talking. Use effective listening.

Those four simple points are very useful for getting people past their fear or self-consciousness. We will develop this idea later in book 2: The 'PEOPLE' Factor.

In-House Communication

Many executives seem to make the mistake of assuming that internal communications programs are not as important as programs they carry out for important external clients. Perhaps it's because they get paid and recognized for one but not the other. As was alluded to earlier, it is the testing of interpretation and understanding by the employees that is of crucial importance. Producing fancy charts showing just how many messages you sent, how many were received and how many were read should cause Constantly Reassess to kick in. Just what do such figures tell you? They certainly do not indicate any meaningful return on investment for the communication since, for example, receiving and opening an email will register as both received and read. Even *if* it was actually read, was it understood? Was it retained? Was it acted upon? How do you know?

Face-To-Face

We have to remember that management is about people. It's about creating, developing and nurturing relationships. It is the experience of human interaction. It is something you cannot fully learn in Business School. We have already touched upon the adage that in organizations information goes up through filters and comes down through loudspeakers. The very existence of such an adage, and the fact that it is true more often than not, should spur you into seeking face-to-face contact with all workers, contacts, and customers on a regular basis. You need to get the real story. As Machiavelli points out:

> By being on the spot, troubles are seen at their birth and can be quickly remedied; not being there, they are heard about after they have grown up and there is no longer any remedy.[133]

There is no way you can ever come to know an employee without having regular face-to-face contact. Résumés and interviews only reveal limited information. Through the 1980s and '90s the conventional wisdom was to take people to restaurants in the hope the social setting would lead to a slipping of the mask. In reality, of course, we cannot do that for every employee. The answer is prolonged face-to-face interactions.

> The old saying 'if you want to know me, then come live with me' can be adapted to the work situation: 'if you want to know your employee then you need to work alongside him/her.'[134]

Technology of course has intruded upon our abilities to meet face-to-face as much as we might otherwise do. There are fantastic benefits from, for example, internet communications. Now, we have the ability to put *the* expert on the job no mater where he or she is. But this should not act as a bar to face-to-face dealings.[135] Imagine the effect you will have if you arrive unannounced to one of the Australian offices, or turn up in Tokyo, or London, or where-ever (we already saw that J.W. Marriott Jr. does this). It is certainly an opportunity you should never let pass. The benefits can be incredible especially if you hold a powerful position in the organizational hierarchy. It can also say a lot to the person you

---

[133] Machiavelli, *The Prince*. P. 10
[134] Humphreys (2006) P. 44.
[135] It will be fascinating watching IT product designers grapple with this problem in the coming years.

drop in on. So long as you take any asshole mentality out from between your ears, you can show how interested you are, how much you care about a project, issue, or person – an unexpected visit can say so much. Manage it properly and it's an investment *not* a cost.

Don't Use a Sledgehammer to Crack a Nut

One of the problems often encountered when people become alert to communication problems is the over compensation that leads to too much. There is absolutely nothing that states more communication equals better communication. As we heard so many times in English class: quality *not* quantity. And I genuinely believe that in the 21st century it is too much communication that is the problem. Emails are too easy to fire around. We copy things on to others with the result that a lot of it really isn't all that relevant. And you can see what's coming: keep firing around nonsense and people start to switch off. Then, when the really important things go around, they ignore them too.

This tendency to email like crazy has led to a bizarre situation whereby the speedy informal attitude that underpinned the concept of emailing has lost most of its charm. Time management books now regularly feature a rule which tells us only to open our emails twice per day. We have, in effect, become victims of our own inabilities to communicate effectively: one of the most efficient methods is now viewed as a barrier to managing our daily tasks.

Of course, some people will view communicating, doing so informally, and managing by walking around as opening the doors to *familiarity breeding contempt* – employees no longer being in awe of the manager – *the tail wagging the dog* – managers viewed as reacting too eagerly to what employees tell them - and curtailing the ability of a manager to *remain slightly aloof*.

First, familiarity only breeds contempt if you refuse to manage the situation. You are not walking around or communicating with people in order to automatically concede concessions, reveal a weakness in yourself or become bullied into doing things you don't want to. The other perspective – the one Constantly Reassess should identify to you - is that you gain respect and build trust since workers come to see that you listen but will not be harassed into anything. They come to see that you can *manage* your interactions.

Second, the tail cannot wag the dog if, again, you manage the situation. Management by walking around includes as much explaining about why you will *not* be acting upon a suggestion as it does about taking a suggestion onboard. Remember, you are a manager. You are listening to *suggestions*, not orders. The fact that you are using the *effective* listening approach means that you are getting behind the words of each suggestion. You are listening with energy, with action. A lot of the time you will be able to show a worker right there and then, through the process of getting behind the words of the suggestion, why it won't fly.

Third, remaining slightly aloof is certainly a quality a lot of people ascribe to leaders. The sledgehammer to crack the nut mentality will not just hear *management by walking around*; it will hear management by *constantly doing nothing other than* walking around. Some maturity, please!

The Power of Silence

Silence is very often golden. It also communicates. When you say nothing, you are actually communicating something to the other person. It might be agreement, disapproval, anything. When an employee doesn't mention something, this may prompt your Constantly Reassess to question whether or not that something is an area requiring some attention.

As humans we are generally uncomfortable with silence especially when dealing with strangers or people we have only known for a short period of time. Any fall off in conversation immediately sees us feeling ill at ease and looking to rush in and fill the void with words, and any words at that. But this is where many of us fall down. Using silence as a strategy is very effective in sales, in conflict resolution – and it is particularly valuable when the other person is holding all the cards.

Let me give you a brief and simplified example. You are earning forty thousand dollars a year. You would love to earn fifty thousand but know there is no chance of your boss giving you a raise above forty two thousand. This, more than likely, is what you will say after your boss asks you the figure you have in mind:

> "I was thinking fifty thousand dollars. Now I know that sounds like a lot and I know that anything above a five percent increase is highly unusual because company norms state between two and four percent and you have to justify costs and stay within budget, but…"

Let's stop there. Can you see what has happened? It's perfectly natural but in just that short opening few words you have handed your boss – count them – at least six reasons to say no:

- ➢ Sounds like a lot;
- ➢ Highly unusual;
- ➢ Company norms;
- ➢ Between two and four percent;
- ➢ Costs;
- ➢ Stay within budget.

You have actually shot yourself down by putting reasons to refuse you into his mouth. Now look at the next version:

> "I was thinking fifty thousand dollars". (Silence).

So now the room has gone quiet and you sit it out. Hardly blinking but sitting looking relaxed and comfortable. First, you have set out your stall. Second, you have not handed the boss reasons to say no. Okay, so perhaps he's thinking you're nuts, you haven't a hope in hell. Fine, but let *him* say that. The more *he* says in return, the more information *he* is giving to you and not vice versa. If he gives reasons for refusing you – negative information – you can take the valuable parts, break them into BabySteps and reply. This works particularly well if the other person seems to be holding all the cards. If you can get them doing most of the talking they can actually hand your argument to you. It may sound highly unprofessional, but it has been my own personal experience that there are lawyers out there who are better in court unprepared than prepared. They go in knowing little or nothing about the case and are therefore open minded about the whole thing. They then simply shoot down every argument put forward by the other side. Strange, but true. Just go back to the example and the six arguments you handed your boss when asking for a salary of fifty thousand. There, had your boss been beamed down from another planet and knew very little, he would win simply by taking your conversation and handing it back to you!

Deepening the Five Constituency Model

Going back to the Five Constituencies, it should be obvious to you that the reactions of each of the Five Constituencies are influenced by numerous factors. For example, each person will have some or all of the following factors bearing down upon them:

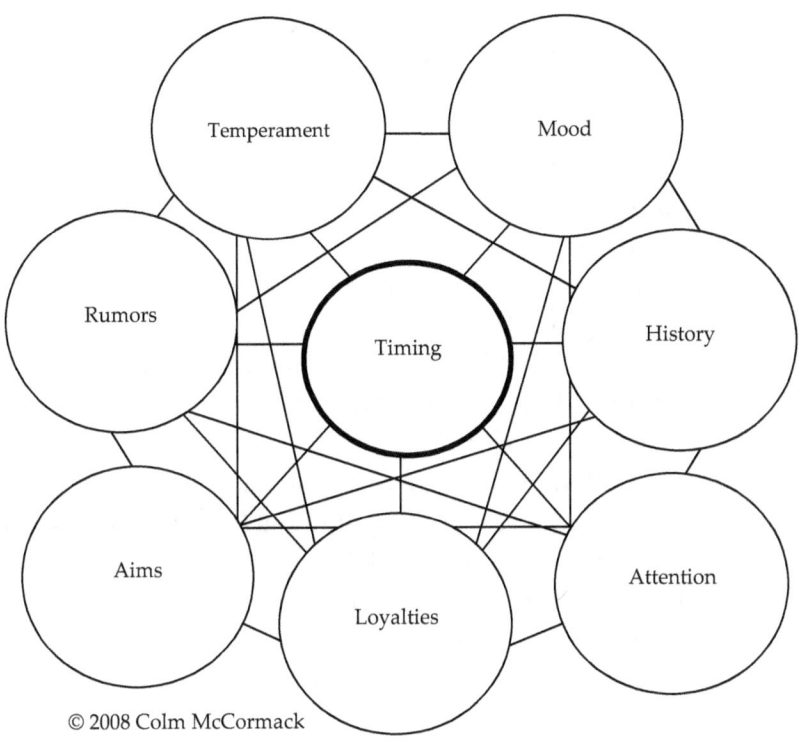

All of these factors are interrelated as depicted in the diagram above. Since this present book – the first in the series – deals specifically with learning to manage yourself, we will return to managing the people around you – and looking in greater detail at the labels in the circles above - in The 'PEOPLE' Factor. [136]

A Brief Communication Effectiveness Assessment

Consider the following questions and then spend the next week keeping them in mind to determine whether or not your

---

[136] Go to: www.JustManageIt.guru for deeper explanation of the diagram above; also see book two of this series: Just Manage It! The 'PEOPLE' Factor: *Leading & Managing the People Around You.*

answers appear to or need to change. I would recommend revisiting these questions regularly – Constantly Reassess:

- Roughly, how would you rate the effectiveness of communication at work and in your personal/home life? When rating the effectiveness, do you have any benchmark to compare your opinion against?
- What easy, subtle, and fast steps do you think you might take to improve the position?
- To whom is blame really migrating for ineffective communications both at work and at home?
- Do you listen at work?
- Do you listen in your personal/home life?
- Do people both at work and at home *know* you are listening? How might they know this? Do you continue reading or watching TV or working at your computer while listening to them? Do you give people your full attention?
- Do you actively listen? Resolve to do this on one occasion every day from now on;
- How often do you interact with key people on a face-to-face basis? Would skipping a layer or two in the organization and communicating face-to-face with those several levels above and below you improve your overall organization vision and understanding? Overall, do you need to increase your face-to-face communications ratio as an individual?
- Do you use silence as a regular part of your communications repertoire? Take note of and reflect upon peoples' reactions and the results you get. Does anyone use this on you? How do *you* react to *their* use of silence?

Some Final Thoughts

How on earth can you hope to manage others if you do not fully understand and cannot manage your own communications repertoire? Spoken words, facial expressions, body language, tone, change in facial color, etc, are all crucial. It is from observing, indulging, reflecting, and experiencing human interaction – not books, models, or frameworks – that we learn, practice, and develop our communication skills. You should take time to chat to as many people as you can face-to-face on a regular basis. Empower yourself by *actively* listening to the people on the front lines and at all different levels throughout the organization. Help yourself by hearing from all stakeholders regularly - listen to your customers, to your employees, get the real story. Seeing someone's expression and demeanor when they chat with you can be so much more informative than chatting on the phone or reading an email. Face-to-face meetings quite often enable you to hear what is not being said. In todays rush toward high-tech everything, it is crucial that in order to rise to the challenge of managing people we actually communicate with people and allow them to communicate with us. It is a human skill, a crucial one. A skill sorely crying out for emphasis within the Business School curriculum but one which, sadly, often goes ignored.

Chapter 7
Context Sensitive

Toward Creating "Context Intelligent" Managers

> Effective leaders are continuously reading the situation and determining how to adapt their behavior to it. They seek to understand the task requirements, situational constraints, and interpersonal processes that determine which course of action is most likely to be successful.[137]

We saw in the last chapter that it was not so much a case of everything leading *to* Communication as springing *from* it. Here, we have a similar situation. I have told you on several occasions of the need to observe others, to watch and listen, to see how they interact with and have an effect on those around them. In other words, in order to manage effectively you must be aware of the context in which you are standing. We must see behavior in context. There is no one-fits-all model or simple answer for managing. This is why we must always investigate first before acting in people issues. Sometimes, otherwise unacceptable behavior becomes acceptable depending upon the context in which it occurs. Hofstede,[138] for example, examined organizational culture in terms of six dimensions. One of them was concerned with whether or not an organization expected workers to conform strictly to the rules and procedures or whether they could act flexibly to meet customers'

---

[137] Yukl (2006) p. 243.
[138] Hofstede, G., et al (1990), *Measuring Organizational Cultures: A qualitative and Quantitative Study across Twenty cases*, in Administrative Science Quarterly 35/2 – referenced from Cole (2004).

needs. Or, in our language, could *context* be taken into account before beating the workers over the heads with the rule book?[139]

We must remember that brilliant work on motivating others can be set at nought if tragedy – whether real or perceived – arrives into a person's life. For them, the context has changed. So context is real *and* perceived. Organizational politics (in fact, all politics) thrives upon perception.

All rules, all principles, all models, all frameworks, all theories, all strategies are subject to this little guiding light - Context. It is from here we derive our *No-one-fits-all* attitude, our *It's all about the timing* rule, and our *it depends* answers. It is from this that the need to activate our internal Constantly Reassess function springs. What works for you today may not work for me tomorrow. The decisions, the things we delegate, what we invest, when, and what we invest in, are all context sensitive. But we generally say, "The timing's not right" instead of "The context is unsuitable".[140] How many times have we heard people referred to as a man or woman of the moment? Could all the great world and business leaders who have gone before repeat their successes now? The odds are against it; the context in which they struck success has lapsed.

For our own present understanding of context and the idea of creating what I term *Context Intelligent* Managers, take a look at the diagram below:

---

[139] For the purposes of our discussion, context will encompass time, timing, and timeliness in addition to circumstances and setting.

[140] Under Sternberg's triarchic theory of intelligence, Sternberg points to the need for adaptation to the environment by combining analytic intelligence, practical intelligence and creative intelligence. (For our present purposes, context intelligent managers must therefore analyze, be practical minded and creative in their analysis and conclusions). See Sternberg, R. (1997). Successful Intelligence. New York. Plume. Sourced from Carr (2004).

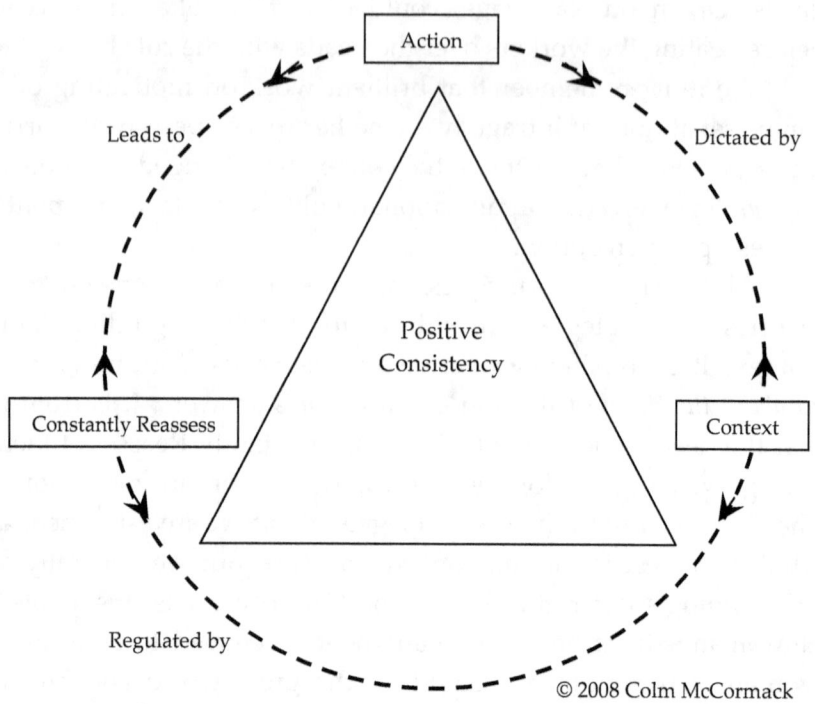

I have constructed this diagram as a summary of some of the items we have covered so far. If we read it in a clockwise direction we will see that Action should be dictated by the Context in which we find ourselves and both the action and context should always be regulated by Constantly Reassess. But we can also read the diagram in the opposite direction: an Action taken should be subject to Constant Reassessment to ensure the Context in which we find ourselves has led us to take the correct action. All of this is Positive Consistency of approach. Be mindful, however, that consistency of approach *does not* equal consistency of results. A change in context, for example, could see you reverse a position. Very often, you will find that people who criticize you for being inconsistent are focusing upon the results and not your consistent approach.

The Ten-Ps of Constituency and Context Awareness

The Five Constituency model is by now more than familiar to you. The entire idea behind the concept is to get you to pause for a brief moment and think beyond yourself. It promotes Constantly Reassess and sets you on the road to Context Awareness. The Ten-Ps that should arise from a meaningful Five Constituency Analysis are depicted in the cycle below:

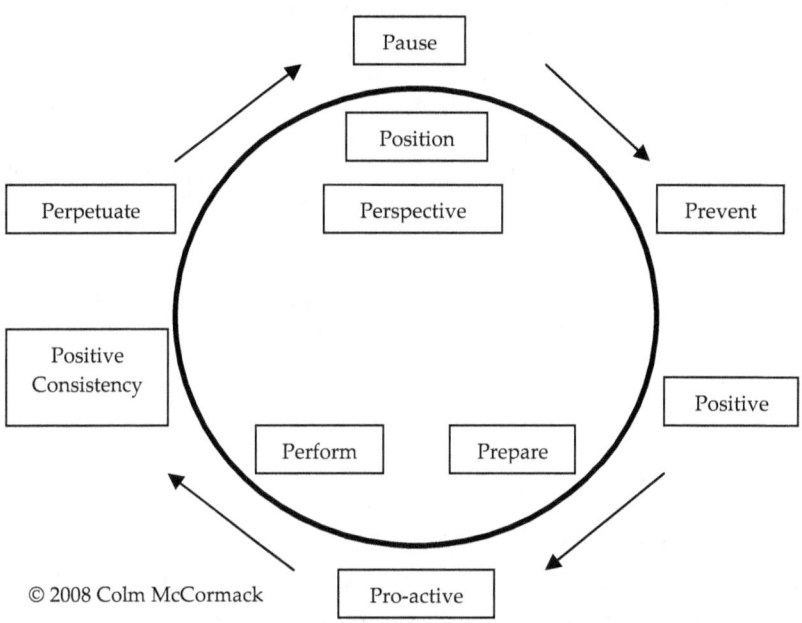

© 2008 Colm McCormack

The meanings I have ascribed to each of the labels, reading in a clockwise direction, are set out in the following table:

Pause	To consider…
Position	Yours and those of others, plus…
Perspective	Yours and the perspective held by others and what that might mean

133

Prevent	First 3-Ps Prevent you from making the wrong Choices thereby increasing/worsening Demands made of you and increasing/worsening the Constraints under which you must operate. Also Prevent Warping of the Psychological Contract (explained later) This in turn leads to…
Positive	Positive attitude, positive perspective, taking an internal locus of control approach, setting suitable examples under an entire process governed by Constantly Reassess
Prepare	The first 5-Ps were preparation: careful consideration of all Five Constituencies.
Pro-Active	The first 6-Ps were Pro-active and Pre-emptory rather than Re-active in nature
Perform	Effective performance should now increase. You have Paused to consider the Position and Perspective, you have Prevented many errors from occurring, can remain Positive going forward under a well-Prepared proactive strategy
Positive Consistency	All of the Ps, if followed, are Positive Consistency in action
Perpetuate	Perpetuating such a cycle will see you taking Action called for by an effective understanding of Context subject to Constantly Reassess - Positive Consistency as depicted in earlier diagram

Assessing Context Comes Easily

We often see children gauging the context of a situation. We continue this during our teenage years. Think back to when you wanted to borrow the car or some money or go on a trip with your pals. You would just be about to ask permission but hear that dad was in a bad mood. So you'd wait until later. (Just like now you check to see if the manager is in a good mood before asking for a pay raise). And why did you put off asking just because dad was in a bad mood? Because by reassessing the situation, you saw that the context had a massive impact upon your odds of success. We know that people can be angrily aroused for more than just a few seconds and that any additional aggravation of an already edgy person can cause trouble (a bit like the way we don't pick our dog or cat up after it's been in a fight). So we come back later. Asking the same person the same question in exactly the same way could lead to polar opposite results. Whether dad said yes or no was Context Sensitive!

But there is something else here that really is truly amazing. Note how by not approaching dad at the wrong moment the kid is focused on the end result *not* all the preparation leading up to it. Yet, when we later graduate to the managerial ranks the opposite is so often the case: we focus on all the preparation, time and cost, and plow ahead ignoring the context – the problem of "Escalation" (spending more and more money, time, and effort on something that has no chance of success simply because the embarrassment or consequences of failure are too great). When you fail to reassess and factor the context into your deliberations then blame must migrate to you should you fail as a result.

Context in Everyday Life

"It depends" is such a classic answer to so many questions or scenarios across a wide range of subjects and topics. But its very utterance reveals an awareness within the human psyche of the importance of context. It shows the person uttering such a remark is assessing context, scenarios, and is aware of the importance of differing approaches to different situations. So we're not talking double-dutch here!

It is from being aware of the context that a lot of the questions featured later in Chapter 8 spring from. As we shall see in the *Are You Running the Green Light?* section, there are times when you have to back down even when you're right. There are times where losing your temper (or at least appearing to do so) is actually appropriate, warranted, and beneficial. Again, it's all about the context in which you are standing.

Change management is hugely context sensitive. Two of the best ways to get people to break from the status quo is impending doom and getting them to discover problems for themselves. These two methods assist in curbing resistance to any change suggested. Many people (and I would be one) advocate implementing change when things are actually going well. Waiting for problems or bad times to arrive is sometimes too late for effective and considered changes to come about. By then, it's all fire-fighting and band aid solutions. But most people resist changing anything when life is all smooth sailing. *If it ain't broke don't fix it* is such a context sensitive defense.

Sales people also know all about the importance of context. There are actually times when you have to refrain from asking for the sale. Sometimes, no matter how desperate you are, you just have to keep your powder dry and wait until the prospect seems more inclined. Irritate him now in the hope of a quick buck and you might lose a potential life-time relationship. Sales, like change, is very context sensitive.

But there's also a flip side to business and context. Some companies make the crazy decision of ramping up their debt levels as a recession seems to be approaching. They then cut advertising and wait until the good times return. Why don't they do the opposite? Ditch your debt as the recession approaches (or at the very least renegotiate more favorable terms) and then advertise through the recession. Then when the good times return, consumers will be dying to throw their new found extra disposable income at your well advertised and newly recognized product or service.

Communication and Context

Communication is context sensitive. Hearing my words to a person as you pass by you might think I'm being harsh, too forward, accusatory. Yet, because the listener and I are involved in a particular situation or conversation, his defensiveness and sense of offence is lowered thereby enabling him to take part in the conversation and hear what I am saying in a different way than an outsider to the conversation might. The opposite is also true. In an argument, people can become highly sensitive to particular words or statements, e.g. you didn't…, you said…, your fault, why didn't you…, and more. As we will see later in the second book of this series – The 'PEOPLE' Factor - what you say and how you say it can have a profound effect upon employees seeking help from their managers. A thorough understanding of communication in context is therefore required for effective management and will be covered in greater detail in book 2.

The 8 Dimensions to Look for in Context

While the following list is certainly not intended to be exhaustive, it is a broad and detailed one that should act as a mechanism to help you minimize the chances of leaving something out of consideration. I have put the list together in the following pie-shaped chart to demonstrate how each interacts to compose context:[141]

---

[141] Time is mentioned in the wheel and at the center of the wheel to signify that it is both a dimension of context in its own right but also an overall governing factor.

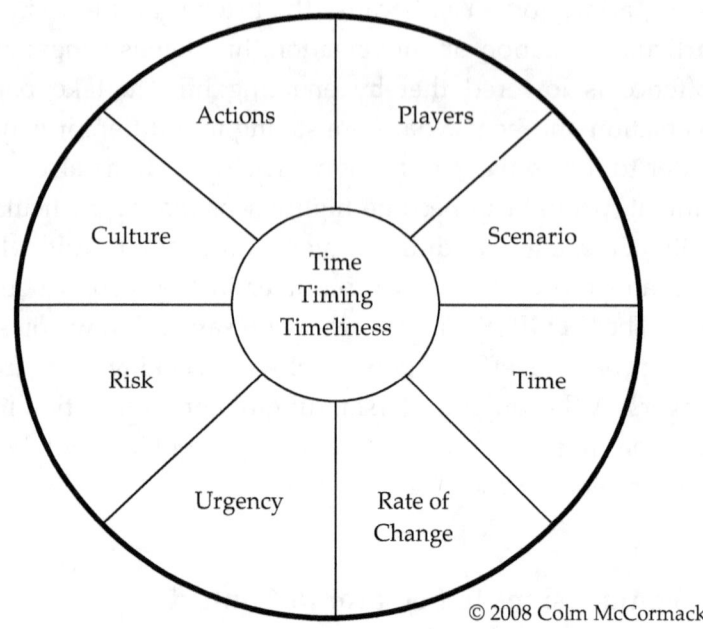

© 2008 Colm McCormack

These 8 items within the chart are now expanded upon in the following table:

Players/People	Who is obviously involved? Who is not obviously involved? Who might be lurking behind the scenes? Who needs to be brought in?
Scenario	What business scenario are you in i.e. product launch, turn around, strike, investigation, conflict, etc?
Time	How long has this scenario been playing out? How long is it likely to last? How might you speed it up or slow it down if required?
Rate of Change	Is the scenario or context changing or do things seem static? How slow or how fast is it changing?
Urgency	How soon must you act, change or reverse a course of action?
Risk	What is the risk of damage if you do act, don't act, act too soon, or act too slowly?

Culture	What is the national, organizational, departmental, floor, team culture? How might this/these impact upon the previous 6 listed items?
Actions	Who is taking action? Who is not taking action? What actions have been taken to date? What actions have not been taken? What actions were considered but then sidelined and why?

The contents of this table enable you to get a more rounded answer to the, "What's going on?" question. Far too often, the answer to such a question is only one or two dimensional, for example, the union has been called in or the product isn't selling as well as it should. Such answers can be greatly and beneficially expanded upon by using the table above to take in more factors for consideration.

At the center of the diagram we saw the words, "Time", "Timing" and "Timeliness". They are expanded upon further in the following table:

Time	All 8 dimensions of Context are subject to Time. They may change or remain the same, change according to set intervals or at random, change in reaction to defined actions or remain unchanged, be greater or lessor affected by the length of time they remain static.
Timing	Observing the 8 dimensions and timing an action, decision, launch, etc, will determine the success or otherwise of your endeavor. Getting the timing wrong will see you introduce your plan into the wrong or a changing context.
Timeliness	An awareness of time and acting at the right moment can all be set at nought if actions and decisions are not governed by timeliness. In other words, you can get so much right but be too slow or too fast in implementing your decision. As there are times when we must act with speed, so too are there times when we must – despite our own frustrations – deliberately act at a slow pace so as not to cause unnecessary change or reaction in and from any of the 8 dimensions.

All the Right Principles in all the *Wrong* Places

It is prudent at this point to sound a warning. So many people read coffee table management books and then adopt a one-fits-all mentality. A lot of the time they haven't fully understood what they have read or miss that they're in a different industry, a different country, and a different company.

It is essential, for example, that as a manager you have a significant degree of flexibility. Where managers go wrong, however, is believing that flexibility extends to the Simple Basics, such as timekeeping, courtesy, etc. It is precisely this misplaced flexibility that can warp the psychological contract against the company, create an unsuitable organizational culture thereby instilling an atmosphere conducive to ineffective and unproductive work.

I have encountered managers talking with the wrong people because they felt they must follow the widely acknowledged principle of consulting with employees. The most alarming problem with this is that in some cases they were actually discussing decisions originally called for due to the behavior of the very people they are discussing the decisions with! You don't consult with all employees in everything.

And consulting takes us to the principle of communicating with employees. Too often communicating becomes an avalanche of unnecessary and irrelevant nonsense. There's a world of difference between too much communication and what Jack Welch advocated as *over communicating* something. Too much is exactly what it says, but over communicating something refers to massive amounts of emphasis upon a small number of points or objectives. The principle is very often over done in the wrong way.

A lot of the time, of course, the practicing of the right principles in the wrong places comes about because of cowardice on the part of the manager concerned. So don't be too quick to label him or her as an idiot. They may just be a coward! I have come across managers who had workers that abused the system, were lazy, etc. Instead of calling the employee to task on it, the managers would start vague conversations with the wrong doers by saying things like, "*How do you think we should go about getting people here to start working properly?*" When everyone knows that John or Mary are free loaders, and John and Mary know it too, then asking John or Mary what to do about it is just going too far. At that point, you're past all that human resource touchy feely nonsense. As I read on a day calendar somewhere along the way: "If you're not fired with enthusiasm you'll be *fired* with enthusiasm!"

We have also come across the idea of managing by walking around. Lots of people adopt this idea but get it so wrong. Remember, it's not the walking around that counts. It's what you're observing, what you're looking and listening for, what you're thinking as you walk around. The aim is not physical but mental exercise.

Many books are now telling us that all employees want is recognition. In fact, the world is starved of it. And that's fine. But where this principle usually goes wrong is the way in which recognition and praise are dished out. We saw in Chapter 1 the dangers of allowing our job title and position to become enmeshed in our sense of identity and self-worth. Now take this concept and apply it to the principle of offering recognition and praise. There's a world of difference between being told, "You're brilliant", and "You did a brilliant job". The first enmeshes the judgment of you with your sense of self-worth. It defines who you are – *you* are brilliant. You will forever try to live up to the brilliant label from that moment onwards. It's one that will lead to more disappointment than anything else. But the "You did a brilliant job" is Context Sensitive. It refers to that thing you did then, in that situation at that moment. Failing at something later, or not doing so brilliant a job on something else, will not lead to you feeling devastated simply because the judgment of you doing that brilliant thing at that moment does not become enmeshed in your self-worth. The judgment does not define who you are.

We must also be careful of the warning that managers must never clone themselves, i.e. hiring people like you can, in the long run, lead to problems. This rule falls down in certain circumstances. For example, when managing change you need supporters. In an extreme situation of dull, unadventurous and resistant employees, being the only one pushing for change will get you nowhere. Cloning yourself in those circumstances by bringing in other like-minded people is not just acceptable: it's advisable and very often crucial for success.

This need to be mindful at all times of the context we find ourselves in highlights again the importance of Constantly Reassess. It is only by reassessing our perspectives, our presumptions, our levels of investigation, our business situation, that we can ever hope to apply the correct approach or solution to any given situation. Reflection and an ability to reassess constantly are required to enable us develop an accurate picture of context. We require the ability to interpret context as experienced by those around us – however unreasonable their views might seem.

Ten Steps to *Ineffectiveness* caused by Context Ignorance

You will remember what I termed the Ten-Ps of Constituency and Context awareness. They were:

> **Pause** to consider **Position** and **Perspective** to **Prevent** you making the wrong choices thereby enabling you to adopt a **Positive**, well **Prepared** and **Pro-active** approach to improve potential **Performance** all of which represents **Positive consistency** and is something you should **Perpetuate** to the benefit of all Five Constituencies since it ensures that Action is dictated by Context and is regulated by Constantly Reassess.

With these ten steps now fresh in mind, take a look at what I term the Steps to Ineffectiveness caused by Context Ignorance. Note the sharp contrast between this and the ten Ps:

Proceed	Pausing rarely happens in any meaningful way;
One-Dimensional View	Positions not properly considered, or only your own and those of a limited few others are considered;
Weakened Perspective	Yours only (and perhaps the perspective of only one or two others) is considered;
No Prevention	A bad start is less likely to prevent you avoiding making the wrong Choices thereby increasing/worsening Demands made of you and increasing/worsening the Constraints under which you must operate. Can lead to you Warping the Psychological Contract (explained later);
Fall off in Positivity	Greater likelihood that your perspective and attitude will be unchanged (at best) or negative (at worst). Only dumb luck or chance can deliver meaningful results;
Poor Preparation	Haphazard (if at all) or totally inadequate due to previous five points listed above;
Lack of Pro-Activity	Nothing in the first 6-Steps here is Pro-active or Pre-emptory;
Performance	Effective performance is now down to dumb luck or unwittingly correct moves. Proceeding without considering all the positions, without viewing the matter from multiple perspectives, and a lack of positive and suitable preparation is begging ineffective results;
Negative Consistency	All of the steps here, if followed regularly, represent consistency: Negative Consistency;
Perpetuate	Perpetuating such a cycle will see you taking Action without an effective understanding of Context and devoid of Constantly Reassess (or reassessing the wrong things). This reaches out to negatively impact on the Five Constituencies, sets unsuitable examples, warps the psychological contract and sees Blame Migrate to you. It also sees you failing to return at the end of the cycle to the issue you began with. Instead, a multitude of differing problems are expected to present themselves all of which eclipse the original issue leaving it unresolved.

These steps are all too familiar to most of us. They seem almost natural and matter of course. In our fire-fighting management style world, the descriptions attached to these labels make a mountain of familiar common sense to any experienced worker. As a manager, it will be your job to break this cycle in the working lives of others but only after you have managed yourself out of the Negative Consistency represented by these steps and into the Positive Consistency of the Ten Ps.

Context Intelligent Managers

It is crucial that business schools release graduates who are context intelligent. The closest most come to teaching this is strategy class where students are told to keep an eye on the external environment and do the occasional in-house cost, resource, systems analysis. But context is vital in life in general. From choosing when to ask dad for the car, to when to ask your spouse something, to when to point something out to one of the children. It's a life skill not just something for use in business. Context comes in a number of phases but for now let's keep it simple: the past, the present, and the future.

How many times have we taken what worked yesterday and tried to stretch it to cover something we're doing today? A lot of the time this will work. But it's the context that is usually the determining feature and not always how brilliantly we implement the idea. Very often, the problem with yesterday is that we judge it using today's criteria. This is very common when criticizing or condemning people. We judge them according to today's rules and laws – rules and laws that didn't apply at the time. In management, the question becomes one of whether or not we can do anything that will reignite the context of yesterday. Can we go back to that place rather than simply taking yesterday's strategy and using it in the wrong era? Or should we take the bare bones of the strategy and amend certain parts to take account of today's context?

We need to take the valuable lessons from the past (both positive and negative) and we must be very aware in our current context of where we are headed to tomorrow. Sometimes we have to hold off from releasing movies or TV adverts because of current sensitivities, e.g. recent disasters or religious issues. Other times, we need to capitalize fast on the emerging context.

When dealing with the future, what's coming down the line? How can you influence it? What criteria do you use? Remember, the quality of your position very often depends upon the quality of the questions you ask.

Some Final Thoughts

Ineffective management and a lack of context intelligence can see us land ourselves in unsuitable contexts of our own making – self-imposed hell if you will. A workers performance today might be a lot poorer than yesterday but perhaps the context has changed. Don't dive into attributing the cause to something internal in the worker. Investigate the circumstances first - if you don't you'll sour the relationship. Make this mistake with enough people and you'll find yourself implementing plans and ideas into a changed context: you'll be implementing things through people whose minds have now turned against you. In other words, your own behavior has changed the context against you.

We can picture the process of moving toward Context Intelligence. We can also picture the process of *retaining* Context Intelligence. And this is important. Learning is a journey, not a destination. So too is development. In fact, we can say leading and managing requires constant learning. Context intelligence is not something you suddenly acquire without any further work required to retain it. A changing context demands that you be proactive to retain an intelligent insight into any new position. I have designed the following model to conceptualize the entire process:

Become →

Focus on	Tools	Process	Result
Players Scenario Time Rate of Change Urgency Risk Culture Action	Observe Analyze Question Actively Listen Interpret Reframe Reflect	Constantly Reassess	Context Intelligence

← Remain

© 2008 Colm McCormack

Note that we focus on the 8 dimensions of context. The tools we use are by now more than familiar to you: they are the building blocks to Constantly Reassess. The entire process of Constantly Reassess moves you toward Context Intelligence. As the diagram also shows, you become and remain context intelligent through Constantly Reassess.

Chapter 8
Questions to Ask Yourself

As we already know, everything is context sensitive: a rule that works today may not work tomorrow. How we act should be dictated by context, but we must also constantly reassess to pick up on any change in context or change in the results expected from our actions. Such a process is positive and therefore referred to as *Positive Consistency*. As was mentioned earlier, so much of the quality around us comes from the quality of the questions we are willing to ask. Asking enables us to Constantly Reassess context, action, results. The following are questions that will take you closer to thinking, reframing, and reassessing quickly on your feet.

Are You Running With The Majority?

> Even today, despite the fact that the world is awash in education and we have the highest levels of intellectual sophistication in history, we cannot seem to escape the perils of a certain kind of irrationality.[142] Men, it has been well said, think in herds; it will be seen that they go mad in herds, while they only recover their senses slowly, and one by one.[143]

---

[142] David J. Schneider (2004) introducing Mackay (1841, 1852).
[143] Mackay (1852).

It is incredible how easily we can be swept along with the tide. This is one of the reasons *Group Think*[144] can have such devastating consequences. Just because everyone agrees on a course of action and are all gung-ho does not mean we should automatically get onboard and go with them. Constantly Reassess should prevent us committing this error. We should be open to information and evidence. We should avoid rationalizing it away and censoring those who bring it to us.

I came across an interesting example with an MBA class. They were sitting in teams and had a project to do. There was some confusion as to various stipulations so the students started chatting with each other about it. Eventually I heard one student remark, *"The others said we do it this way…"* There they were, the so-called leaders of tomorrow, on the verge of potentially setting off in the wrong direction. And yet everyone was perfectly happy and comfortable with this because there was no sense of being alone in the endeavor – Social Proof in full action. Just think about what they were about to do. They were prepared to act in a certain way together but to what illogical end? To later fight with the faculty in some bizarre hope that the sheer weight of numbers would make them surrender and conclude: "Well, so many people getting it wrong must mean they're right and we should ignore all stipulations to the contrary"? What they were actually doing without realizing it was deliberately setting themselves up to fail with a belief that sticking together would turn the wrong way of doing something into the right way.

We see this too in the world of investments. If so many people are investing in a stock or in property, then it must be the thing to do, right? How often do we see this mistake? Herd mentality may

---

[144] In broad terms, Group Think is a theory referring to the way in which a highly effective group can start to become ineffective without any obvious reason. There are eight symptoms that can point to the emergence of Group Think (see work of Irving Janis on the subject).

work on the Serengeti where only one or two get picked off and killed. But in the business world, the entire herd gets eaten!

Are You Running the Green Light?

My grandmother always warned us about this: driving your car through a green light and proceeding despite another guy running his red light. Simply doing so because you have the right of way can lead, as she would say, to you being right, but dead! This works too in the work setting. I wish I had a dollar for every time I saw a manager start a war with a regular member of staff but looking stupid at the end of the day despite having been right. It is things like these that start conflict, set unsuitable examples and shatter morale.

The best advice I can give you on this point is to echo the words of my late father:

> "If you feel you must constantly impose your authority, you obviously don't have any".

This takes us to a question we should ask ourselves occasionally: "Am I taking myself too seriously?" Asking yourself this question is Constantly Reassess in action. Since we know that All Blame Migrates, running the green light but later trying to blame others for the unhappy atmosphere that arises simply won't work.

Are You Making an Attribution Error?

If you look you will see this everyday, either in yourself, others, or both. What is an attribution error? It is wrongly interpreting the causes behind a person's behavior to internal factors within that person or to factors external to them. A good example is labeling someone as lazy just because they arrive late to work two or three days in a row. You instantly conclude an internal laziness within the person is the reason, but might it be something outside their control? Or consider a salesman making less calls than his peers being labeled unfocused by others without ever considering any factors external to the person, for example, he might have greater distances to travel per call than his peers.

At best we blame people for the doings of others or circumstances beyond their control. At worst, we are blaming people for things we ourselves cause. Think of the salesman who has to travel farther than the rest of his team and therefore makes fewer calls per day. If *we* assigned that area to him, then we are doubly wrong in assuming something within the salesman himself (e.g. laziness or lack of focus) is the cause. *We* are the cause in that example and Blame Migrates to us.

Jumping the gun, jumping to conclusions, assuming the worst in everyone and (worst of all) voicing these concerns without first checking, gathering proof or considering you yourself might be the cause, are things you need to be very alert to. This calls Constantly Reassess back into action and brings suitable example-setting very much to the fore.

Under LMX Theory (we looked at this earlier) the manager's in-group generally find things going their way. If they fail, the manager will make an external attribution, i.e. he will blame something outside of the worker for the problem e.g. not enough resources, the system, etc. The in-group also gets praised when they get things right. But the out-group members get the opposite treatment. When they succeed, the manager assumes it was something external to them, e.g. him! When they fail, it was them! After all, that's why they're not in the in-group right? Because they're stupid! What a life – no support but all of the blame. Attribution errors are very common![145]

Are You Warping the Psychological Contract?

A psychological contract is simply the unspoken rules or agreements that exist in the work place.[146] For example, your boss never tells you that if you work hard you'll go far, but there is that silent recognition and acceptance between you both. The majority of books I have come across on this topic all seem to focus upon a question of whether or not one exists in a particular organization. In fact, exams and assignments regularly ask:

> Is there a psychological contract in place in your organization? Give examples to backup your answer.

It is my view that there is *always* a psychological contract, and in badly run companies such contracts can be counter productive. It is my contention that as a manager, you can warp the psychological contract against the company (in fact, against *all* Five Constituencies) through your behavior and lack of positive action. Think about:

- Good workers (constituency 2) around the poor worker who get no recognition or extra reward and who get the same pay rise and bonus as the poor performer;
- The overall effect this has upon the organization itself (constituency 3) since the good workers throughout the organization are watching all of this and it impacts them psychologically, emotionally, and motivationally;

---

[145] Perhaps such constant behavior should see us amend the phrase to "Attributional Habits".
[146] Gunnigle et al (2002).

- ➤ The seepage of resulting poor mood, attitude, climate and culture out to external stakeholders (constituency 4);
- ➤ The bad worker (consitiuency 1) continually getting away with it and consciously deciding to continue in the same mode;
- ➤ A company suddenly deciding to get these bad workers moving again.

The last point is the most volatile. It is the kick in the ass you will receive and deserve when the bad workers engage in a backlash against change and will no doubt lead to accusations of victimization, stress, and bullying. The other points are the reasons why you *must* act. Not doing so is why a company can crumble slowly from the inside out. The good workers will leave and the managers could, theoretically, be left with a house of crap!

What we are seeing here is a link to Positive Consistency. When this is absent, the psychological contract comes under huge strain and can warp against the company very easily. Once this happens, it is unlikely that matters will ever return to the desired state. There is ample scope to argue that there is no such thing as a restoration of a good position. Once lost it is gone forever so the "return" is in fact a *new* position. This likely outcome calls into focus the need to Constantly Reassess your assumptions, perspectives and attitudes. A warping of the psychological contract is fertile ground for conflict.

Are You Measuring Everything?

One of the simple truths of management is that you can't measure everything. Some things are just intangible, or would require an army of researchers, statisticians and marketers to commit them to paper. The trick when this happens is to come up with a system. It doesn't have to be mathematically perfect so long as our friend Consistency enters the fray. Imperfect systems of measurement can still be useful if used consistently since any variance will still show up. An every day classic mistake on the measurement and consistency front can be seen when people are cooking. They will look at the clock on the wall when putting a meal in the oven but then quite often use their wrist watch, or alternate between the two, during the cooking period. This might seem trivial, but how many arguments have broken out in team rooms when one person is judged by the rest to be late only for the late comer to show the time on his/her watch to others to prove he/she is not actually late?

Think of the simple examples. I might be running a small privately owned company and want some indication of its performance relative to other companies. I could look at the profit margins of the top five quoted companies in my industry and get an average of the five. Then, perhaps, add on a few points to reflect the fact that the big guns really know what they're doing, have economies of scale, bulk buying power, etc. Then I stick with the Consistency principle and use that form of measurement every year – always taking the average of the top five and adding on the same number of points to reflect the size of my little business. Not perfect, but adequate, and reinforced by Positive Consistency.

A great yet simple example is given by Robert Sutton.[147] He details a company which decided to measure the cost it was incurring as a result of one unsuitable sales person. The company measured the time spent by the employee's direct manager, the HR professionals, the senior executives, the company's outside employment counsel, the cost of recruiting and training a new secretary for the employee, the overtime costs that flowed from his last minute demands, etc. Not mathematically water tight, but a

---

[147] Sutton (2007)

good indicator of what was going on and an approach that can be used consistently in the future. Sutton makes an interesting point:

> ...no matter how compelling your stories and lists of drawbacks might be, people from accounting, finance, and other quantitative backgrounds often rule the roost, and they seem to prefer to make decisions on the basis of bad (even useless) financial estimates rather than no estimates at all. So it might be wise to use the language they want to hear, no matter how rough the estimates.[148]

What you really need to keep in focus is that failing to manage something simply because you cannot see a way to measure it will eventually see blame for any resulting negative consequences migrating to you. You cannot sit on our hands chanting "but I don't know how to do it", for long. Ask people. Go to your external network if need be. Manage it!

Are You Suffering from Favor Blindness?

I want to break favors out of the general list of items to be measured. Here we revisit our friend Positive Consistency again. It really is one of the golden rules of management. You would probably be shocked at just how fast favors mount up over the length of a year or term of a contract.

I woke up one day and realized lots of people were making money from advice I would give them. But I wasn't getting a penny.[149] Emails, phone calls, meeting for a drink or two. People would ask me questions during a conversation. Then weeks later I'd hear they changed something along the lines of what we had discussed. They'd make a small fortune and I'd still be sitting there

---

[148] p. 41. Useful considering our earlier discussion on Communication. Sometimes you simply must speak *their* language. So, to convince marketers, accountants, or strategists, you must speak marketing, numbers, or strategy in order for there to be effective and meaningful communication.

[149] Anyone who works for free will always be busy!

on skid row. I was doing favors for people but getting nothing in return – negative consistency in behavior on my part. I've also seen this up close and personal in several companies along the way. Take an insurance company for example. Sometimes in order to keep large clients on side, the underwriters will cover small claims that are not strictly covered under the terms of the policy. Yet, small amounts can add up to a nasty surprise. But it's not just a cost issue. The point is consistency, empowerment, and an avoidance of conflict. How?

Good management, as we have seen, will automatically call for Positive Consistency. If you are keeping a record of all favors you do for a given client, then you have empowered yourself or, more to the point, you have not given your power away. When the client comes looking for a better deal when the contract is up for re-negotiation, your record of favors puts you in a very strong position since you can show – in an extreme case - that a significant percentage of the original contract price was actually refunded to the client via the favors.[150] It has been my experience that the monetary value of some companies habit of doing favors can come to seriously worrying amounts when measured against the overall value of the contract itself. [151]

And negotiations are an important topic when discussing measuring your favors. Trained negotiators – in an effort to avoid having to reciprocate – will often devalue the concessions of an opponent. This can see a lot of concessions going unacknowledged and with little or no reciprocation resulting. Remember this when dealing with your employer, with clients, with people. You need to let people know the size of the favor and the cost where appropriate. You need to keep track of this. Research has shown that the recipients of favors view them as important when received

---

[150] Also shows a value to the relationship from the client's perspective.
[151] Too many companies place themselves on the brink of rendering clients unprofitable through the absence of careful monitoring backed up by activity-based accounting.

but this view decreases with time. Those granting the favors, however, view them as unimportant at first but the importance grows with time.[152] And there's a warning for women here too. Women have been shown – in general – to be less likely to ask for pay increases than men.[153] If this weakness spills over into seeking the return of favors – or using a record of favors done to empower oneself or stem the tide – then there could be problems ahead.

If you refuse to keep track of the favors that all of your employees extend to clients then any loss suffered as a result, and your lack of power in contract renegotiations, will see blame migrating to *you* for failing to put a system of recording and measurement in place. Sometimes your secretary or personal assistant will dip into your personal pool of favors for a family member or friend without you even realizing it. Little things, for example, good seats at a restaurant, tickets to an event – things your assistant can easily do but which is score-carded by others without you even realizing what is going on.[154]

As for conflict, keeping a record of favors avoids conflict since recorded facts cannot be argued with. This will also make in-house life for staff easier. Positive Consistency really is a true and loyal friend.

---

[152] Goldstein et al (2007).

[153] See: Babcock, Linda and Laschever, Sara. *Women Don't Ask – Negotiation And The Gender Divide*. (2003). Princeton University Press.

[154] I am always amazed how the members of new bands each leave a list with the front door or ticket office of a paying gig. These lists contain names of pals to be let in for free. When they're starting out expecting a crowd of 300 with five band members leaving a list of ten to twenty names each, they're eating into their margins in a serious way. Measuring these favors as a group should act as a useful wakeup call and alert the band early to nonsensical management practices.

Are You Being Fooled By The Numbers?

I remember agreeing to help a small struggling company. The accountant emailed five years of the company accounts to me and I sat down to do the analysis, ratios and all that other brilliant stuff. You can almost hear the conclusions now: grow sales, cut costs, lower the inventory numbers, improve the cash flow...etc. Sales *and* distribution were handled by an independent distributor contracted by the company. It was obvious: if sales were down whip or ditch the distributor since he had taken on the dual sales-distribution function. After all, it was right there in the numbers: he wasn't performing and we were suffering as a result. Growing revenues by upping sales was starting to look like a serious mistake. Why? After several meetings with people out in the real world I began to discover we had little, if any, brand recognition. Our labels were not entirely effective, the people selling our products knew nothing about them, there was no advertising...the list went on and on. Whipping the distributor to grow sales would have been like ordering him to get more blood out of an already well-bled stone. The numbers had me focused on the symptoms and *not* the cause. Upping sales was not the *action* – it would be the *result* from other key actions such as focusing on brand, etc. Organizations generally operate as sets of functions. Financial ratios tell you very little. There are cross-functional synergies at work that ratios cannot pick up on.

There are two very important observations to take from this little experience. First, don't be afraid (or too lazy) to look behind the numbers. Yes, they are showing you *what* is happening (e.g. you're losing money) but not necessarily *why*. The second lesson should be obvious: listen to your customers. By going behind the numbers and listening to the customers, the retailers, the distributor, I was able to find out what was really going on. Prepare to get creative if you're not a big hitter, and listen to everyone who takes the time to talk to you about your business, your products, your services.

Are You Managing the Right Things?

Take a look at your own job in the coming days. Why do you do the things you do? Might you have inherited tasks from your predecessor that really shouldn't be your problem? Was it a case of *do a man a favor and it soon becomes your job*? For example, if you fixed the photocopier one time, or ordered toner, do people now mention *your* name when the photocopier gives up the ghost or toner runs out? Are you weak on the saying *No* front? Are you afraid to delegate? Are you a glory hunter who wants to keep the great projects for yourself even if someone else can do them better, faster? Do you have trust issues when it comes to giving others tasks or delegating to them? If so, why? Did you neglect training people so they could do these things? Is blame migrating back to you when answering all of these questions?

When we look at the sub-prime loans fiasco we generally look at the symptoms and not the cause. The cause is the inability of people to do the simple money management basics – something they were never taught in school. This problem of managing the wrong thing also extends to everyday issues such as overeating, for example. Chronic overeaters on weight loss programs can lose a hell of a lot of weight. But at some point they must stop losing weight or they risk going too far. And that's where the problems usually kick in. As soon as they start eating again they pile all the weight back on. Why? Because nobody ever dealt with the actual problem. They all saw being over weight as the symptom and overeating as the cause. Wrong. Over-eating is the symptom:

there's something lying deep beneath the surface that needs to be addressed.[155] In other words, they were managing the wrong thing.

Do You Focus as Good as You Should?

One of the key indicators that a person cannot manage themselves properly is a tendency to run around scatterbrained. You will see this everywhere. A very good friend of mine is a successful General Manager at a reputable brokerage in Dublin, Ireland. He is used to me giving him a hard time over how he never does within a five day week what he says he will do. I worked with him for a few months. I would tell him we need something and he would reply, "I'll do it now". The following week I would notice he hadn't done whatever it was he said he'd do. And this happens with everything he does. It's simply a low threshold for distraction coupled with poor focus. On the way to his desk someone would say something, or he'd see something and that thing would knock the current task out of his mind. He never wrote things down. The best way to give you a clear insight into this subtle yet potentially devastating managerial deficiency is to quote an email that has been doing the rounds for years:[156]

> I decide to water my garden. As I turn on the hose in the driveway, I look over at my car and decide it needs washing. As I start toward the garage, I notice mail on the porch table that I brought up from the mailbox earlier. I decide to go through the mail before I wash the car. I lay my car keys on the table, put the junk mail in the garbage can under the table, and notice that the can is full. So, I decide to put the bills back on the table and take out the garbage first. But then I think, since I'm going to be near the mailbox when I take out the garbage anyway, I may as well pay the bills first. I take my check book off the table, and see that there is only one

---

[155] How interesting it would be if it ultimately transpires that years of cancer research later reveal cancer to be the symptom and not the cause.
[156] My apologies to whoever penned this mail: I quite simply do not know who it was so cannot therefore give them due credit for their brilliance.

check left. My extra checks are in my desk in the study, so I go inside the house to my desk where I find the can of Coke I'd been drinking. I'm going to look for my checks, but first I need to push the Coke aside so that I don't accidentally knock it over. The Coke is getting warm, and I decide to put it in the refrigerator to keep it cold. As I head toward the kitchen with the Coke, a vase of flowers on the counter catches my eye--they need water. I put the Coke on the counter and discover my reading glasses that I've been searching for all morning. I decide I better put them back on my desk, but first I'm going to water the flowers. I set the glasses back down on the counter, fill a container with water and suddenly spot the TV remote. Someone left it on the kitchen table. I realize that tonight when we go to watch TV, I'll be looking for the remote, but I won't remember that it's on the kitchen table, so I decide to put it back in the den where it belongs, but first I'll water the flowers. I pour some water in the flowers, but quite a bit of it spills on the floor. So, I set the remote back on the table, get some towels and wipe up the spill. Then, I head down the hall trying to remember what I was planning to do. At the end of the day: the car isn't washed the bills aren't paid there is a warm can of Coke sitting on the counter, the flowers don't have enough water, there is still only one check in my check book, I can't find the remote, I can't find my glasses, and I don't remember what I did with the car keys. Then, when I try to figure out why nothing got done today, I'm really baffled because I know I was busy all day, and I'm really tired.

You'd be amazed just how many people actually think like this. I see it every time I observe managers and supervisors going about their daily tasks. This email is certainly humorous but there is something in it that is familiar to all of us. The solution is simple. It's just like everything else in this book: it takes a little time and a little bother. A lot of people refuse to work on such deficiencies because they're too busy. Yep, too busy running in circles as a result of *this* managerial deficiency.

If you're going to manage yourself and meet the demands made of you, then choose not to allow your own focus deficiency act as a constraint upon yourself and those around you. Stick to a task and get it done. Take notes of other things along the way to ensure you return to them. Prioritize. Focus. Complete. Move on.

Are You An "...or..." Person?

I simply cannot understand people who seem to go out of their way to make life hard for themselves. Usually it's out of fear of rejection or fear of imposing, but the use of "or" when making a request can be a huge problem. Let me give you an example. How often have you heard something like this:

"Can you send me a copy of that article...or...are you too busy today?"

The question mark *should* pop up after the word "article", but instead the "or" enters to (1) lengthen the sentence; (2) to give the listener a way out of committing; (3) to greatly increase the odds of you receiving a disappointing result. My advice to people is always this:

- State what you want and then stop. Shut-up. Don't go any further and don't drop the "...or..?" onto the end of your sentence;
- Stop giving people a way out. If they want to refuse then let *them* find the door away from making a commitment;
- Use peoples' general inability to say "No" against them.

So, "Can you send me a copy of that article...or...are you too busy today?" now becomes, "Can you send me a copy of that article please". Polite, short, and to the point, with or without it being phrased as a question, not giving them a way out but instead placing the onus on *them* to come right out and either refuse or give a reason as to why not or why there might be a delay in meeting your request. Far too many people see this suggested approach as bullying or impolite. But this is only true if you carry it out in an overly direct and/or threatening manner. Even, "Send me a copy of that article when you get back to your desk. I'd love to take a closer look at it", is far more effective than the overly-polite and lame request punctuated with the "or". Again, if the person does not want to send it to you, it is up to them to say so.

Do You Understand the Words? Have You Got the Right Perspective?

One of the first issues we came across was the perspective that problems should not equate to unhappiness. Life is not a problem-free zone. Remember, it is you who is in control of your feelings and emotions. Problems are opportunities to learn, to Constantly Reassess, to change course. They are only to be expected so get to dealing with them when they arise rather than sitting around complaining about them.

We might say that rejection in life is not always a problem: often it's the fear of rejection that holds us back. As we saw earlier in Chapter 2, the real enemy is the status quo. But fear of our ideas, our plans – whatever – being rejected causes us to reinforce the status quo. In other words, we strengthen the enemy through our inaction. As the saying goes, anticipation of death is worse than death itself. So it is with fear of rejection. In business and management – in life in general – rejection is part of the game. You'll feel disappointed, maybe even a little down for a while, but it's rarely as bad as your imagination painted it out to be prior to you acting.[157]

One of the most devastating mindsets emanates from the United States where so many children are raised to "be the best". How often have we heard this backed up with nonsense like, "first or nothing", "nobody ever remembers who came second"? As we

---

[157] As I read somewhere along the way: If you're ever afraid to try something new just bear in mind that amateurs built the Ark but professionals built the Titanic!

saw, allowing the opinions and attitudes of others to determine the way in which we view and value ourselves equates to giving power over how we feel to others. That is not the way to go. Each of us controls (or should) our own feelings and emotions. The trick is always to aim for doing *your* best not to be *the* best on the planet.[158] Remember this: do *your* best, don't aim to be *the* best in everything. And for God sake, pass this perspective to your children too!

I am a great believer in moving away from "right" and "wrong" and instead substituting "suitable" and "unsuitable" (people use "effective" and "ineffective" in the world of therapy). To declare something as the *wrong* way to act must surely mean that it is always wrong. The word *wrong* introduces permanency to our thinking. So too does the word *right*. Both words suggest an ignorance of context sensitivity.

There is a difference between confrontation and conflict. It is also important to note the difference between friend and friendliness. It is the former that can cause so many problems. We race into new jobs and try to be friends with everyone. We fall into the aim of being liked. The trick of course is to have a mix of the two (being liked and being respected) and to focus upon being *friendly* as opposed to being friends. Women, generally speaking, because of their relationship-focused nature, can fall into this trap of wanting to make friends and then feel devastated when the feelings are not reciprocated.

Competence and perfection are not the same things. Neither are motivation and manipulation. Nor delegation and abdication. Nor loyalty to a company and slavery to it. Yet it is amazing just how many times we pick the wrong one in each of the paired choices. Refusing to work eighteen hours a day, for example, and

---

[158] This should of course be tempered occasionally by some outside benchmarking or brief referral to others in order to properly motivate and introduce a sense of stretching performance. Doing your best will not therefore be viewed as surrender, taking the easy way out, or failing to reach your full potential.

being labelled "disloyal" by your boss is a nonsense. It has nothing whatsoever to do with your loyalty. You are simply refusing to be a slave. But, as with watching for excuses masquerading as reasons, we also have to watch out for word play and perspective twisting by others. Sometimes – tragically – we do these things to ourselves. Organizational life is full of people who actually have the incorrect understanding of words in their heads.

Are You a Victim of the Age & Experience Trap?

At what stage in a man's life does he go to bed on a Sunday night with insufficient experience and wake up on Monday morning with just the right level of experience? When any of us are looking for an experienced person, what exactly do we mean? We might stipulate 10 years in a senior management position but then come across a person who was only a team leader but held that position at one of the major corporations like McKinsey or GE. When that happens, you can bet the 10 year stipulation starts to slide. Farm the job out to an employment agency that simply ticks the boxes, however, and you're missing a world of talent.

It is not simply the case that some of the biggest names out there got to where they are because they are exceptional people. That's a cop-out. The big guns are where they are because along the way *other people* made exceptional decisions that opened doors for them. Think about it. Was Jack Welch appointed General Manager at the age of 32 and Michael O'Leary appointed CEO of Ryan Air because they were exceptional managers? Maybe, but the *real* reason they were appointed was because somewhere somebody had the guts to make an exceptional decision to appoint them. Your employer has a role to play in making certain you succeed in your new position and/or new industry. Adopting a sink or swim attitude is idiotic. It will cost him time and money. Make it your mission to prove his doubts wrong.

There is nothing which states that *all* of your knowledge and expertise must come from having lived the experience yourself. This is why business schools have case studies and guest speakers: so that the sharing of experiences can provide shortcuts to valuable insights and knowledge. There is simply not enough time to experience everything for yourself so books, conversation, shared insights, are all crucial tools for the modern manager.

Looking for experience and experience alone excludes attitude, enthusiasm, objectivity, fresh outlook, ability to actually do the job.... the list goes on. So don't let people beat you up over a lack of experience. Remember, experience demands mistakes, is costly, takes time, is unforgiving, can teach the wrong things, and can produce one-trick-ponies. Studies have also found that lower aged top management teams with high education, varied backgrounds and who were relatively new to their organizations were better able to facilitate corporate change.[159] Nor, however, should you confuse knowledge and sharpness in college with wisdom. A lack of experience still has its place if marshalled correctly.

> If you can lead and manage a plastics business, you should be able to run an aerospace or a financial services business.[160]

Here is the way you *should* approach a top job even if you are coming from another industry:

> ➤ You should arrive with your old network and an additional network of external advisors in place. Changing industry does not automatically render these networks null and void.

---

[159] Wiersema & Bantel (1991). See Journal of General Management 2001 for an account of the Turbo Project run by Belgacom, the Belgian telephone company which based its project on the findings of Wiersema & Bantel.
[160] *Leadership Development for Small Organizations*. Marshall Tarley, March 2002, pg 55.

They are simply reduced in terms of relevance but relevant still nonetheless;
- Your employer has made a significant investment in taking you on. Don't allow him to simply throw you into the deep end in the hope you will swim. Ask for the names of twelve or so people he knows you should contact inside and outside the organization to aid a successful transition into your new role;
- If you are worth hiring, you will have arrived to each interview already having researched the company, the industry, its rivals, etc. So, you are not as ignorant as he might suppose. In fact, you might just have a better understanding of the company's position than a lot of the current senior managers. Build upon this by sitting down with him and designing an eighty to ninety day transition period. During this period, you will adjust your own previous network and advisory network, you will contact the names he gave you and build your own internal network within the organization. You will also set about learning the technical aspects as they pertain to the organization and its industry sector;
- Build upon this by asking for specific and targeted training. If he leaves you to learn for yourself, you might miss something or spend too much time focusing upon the irrelevant;
- Work on your conceptual and interpersonal skills. You are already working upon their technical skills but it is the conceptual and interpersonal skills that top managers rely upon heavily;
- Ask that training be made a constant feature. This is something he should already be doing. Expecting excellence to walk through the door and retain its own shine forever is a faulty perspective.

Now things should start to look somewhat different. He has gone from a perspective of not hiring you because you didn't have enough experience to a perspective of hiring a good manager and seeing you up and fully running within eighty to ninety days of starting your new job. He has made an exceptional decision to hire a real asset and unlocked its potential by pro-actively nurturing, training and developing it.

> If you have joined an industry you are not familiar with, you should be able to pick up the key issues within a few weeks at most, and you must know whom to ask if you need to find out specifics. There is a huge benefit, in fact, to coming in from a fresh angle. The very fact you don't know much gives you the ability to question why things are done in a particular way. Turn your lack of knowledge to your advantage.[161]

A one month interviewing period plus a 90-day settling in period will put any sharp person at the top of their game along with others who have spent years in that particular industry or sector. Machiavelli makes an interesting observation in relation to age and experience and my argument that any potential candidate worth their salt will have completed a lot of preparatory work before taking up the post:

> ...states that arise quickly, just like all the other natural things that are born and grow rapidly, cannot have roots and branches and will be wiped out by the first adverse weather. This occurs unless the men who have suddenly become princes...possess such virtue that they know how to prepare themselves rapidly to preserve what Fortune has dropped into their laps, and to construct afterwards those foundations others have laid before becoming princes.[162]

But we must also remember that your experience can be invisible. This can be a strong problem for women who display and

---

[161] Robinson (2004) pg 178
[162] Machiavelli: *The Prince*, p. 24

exercise leadership in several roles outside of work without taking credit for it. So many of the things people do in life never seem to register on the *experience* radar. Sometimes our hobbies, caring for a dieing loved one, sitting on neighborhood or school boards, etc, give us invaluable experience and expertise. Take a look at the following excerpt:

> ...a woman wrote us to say "After researching my son's chronic illness for the last five years, I would like to go into medical information research, but I don't have any experience". Obviously, she had considerable experience, but she was discounting the experience she had because she didn't have any formal academic or on-the-job training.[163]

The inconsistency in criteria for selecting people was well demonstrated by a story that was related to me in the course of researching this book. An MBA graduate, with marketing experience in the UK, applied to a drinks giant for a marketing job in Ireland. She was refused on the grounds she didn't have enough experience of doing the exact same job in Ireland! She returned to London and did some temping work. While there, the company she was temping for was appointed to do work by the drinks giant, but a marketing manager would have to be appointed by the London company. Guess who they picked? Yep, the lowly temp. The drinks giant never objected to the person they said wasn't good enough now landing the role she had originally applied for. Do you see anything strange in all of this? Not only do companies hold contrasting sets of criteria, they can unwittingly ignore them too.[164]

---

[163] Edwards & Edwards and Douglas (1998).
[164] We can also see that the London company got it right: they weren't afraid to pick someone from the bottom of the pile and place her where her talents could be used to great effect.

Perriscope Up – Where Are We?

Over the last few chapters, we have slowly moved toward making Constantly Reassess our new automatic default setting. Reframing, looking to see if Context is right, looking to see whether or not conflict is useful, whether our work and personal lives are both being managed effectively toward a better overall result, looking to see if we have the right Reference Group in focus, looking at the Demands, Constraints and Choices in our lives, looking at how we use our time…and more – all of these things are Constantly Reassess returning as a positive habit and action. You can now add to this by doing the following:

- You should ask yourself the question, "Am I taking myself too seriously?", on a regular basis especially when ever you feel deadlock or an argument or disagreement is about to take place;
- Constantly look to see whether or not your actions are truly dictated by the actual context in which you are standing (or about to enter) and whether or not that context is truly regulated by a deliberate attempt to Constantly Reassess;
- Watch over the coming days and weeks for instances where others (and you too) might be running with the crowd rather than pausing to investigate matters briefly;
- From now on be aware that being right will not always lead to you being viewed by others as winning. Consider how proceeding despite this knowledge – and knowing full well that others are watching – will impact upon the Five Constituencies;
- Refrain from jumping in to solve problems or deal with people without first investigating the matter. Move away from making incorrect attributions about the people around you. A little time up front will save you a lot of time later.

You need to start watching for actions or perceptions that might warp the organizational psychological contract against you and the organization;
- Consider carefully the various things you have *not* been measuring. Start! If you don't know how to measure something – ask;
- Start measuring your favors from today onwards. Don't become petty or personal;
- Resolve to get behind the numbers your accountant is presenting to you. Meet with customers. Talk with employees. Meet with suppliers and distributors. Talk with competitors
- Go back over your last few hires and see can you determine whether or not you or the organization has fallen into the Age and Experience Trap. Sit down with your HR Director or your recruitment agency and discuss this issue. Ask the following questions when looking at previous hires:
    - Did we adopt a sink or swim attitude toward the person?
    - How did we/you help each of the last hires?
    - When you yourself were hired to your job, what help did you get?
    - What small, subtle steps could you take to improve this situation?
- Watch to see if you are using the "…or…" in your questions and requests: stop boxing yourself in.

Chapter 9
*Every*body Sets an Example

> "People the world over have always been more impressed by the power of our example and not the example of our power."[165]

So far we have looked at ourselves. We've looked at the idea of managing ourselves before trying to manage others. We have explored the idea of putting our lives in order, on a desirable track. We have become aware of many of life's and management's pitfalls – blame, a lack of responsibility, wrongly placed locus of control, negativity in thinking and in the people around us. Becoming aware of such issues enabled us to reflect upon them in our own lives, how they impact upon us. We then looked outward to the rest of the world – we started observing others. Unsuitable behavior in others allowed us to regulate our own behavior and reinforce the positives. By observing a person at the center of the Five Constituency model, we can then imagine ourselves at the center under observation thereby reflecting and learning from the experiences of observation. We should also be starting to see a lot of what is actually behind the behavior of others. So instead of diving in to manage a situation, we are starting to understand the people - unearthing their motivations, discovering their direction of focus, and perhaps even coming to gain insights they don't yet have into themselves.

---

[165] Former U.S. President Bill Clinton.

But of course resistance is out there in the form of other people. So too are objection and resentment.[166] We will now move in this chapter toward gently bringing people along with us without rounding them up, without forcing silly projects or programs upon them.[167] By managing our own lives we now allow this to seep out and affect others in a highly positive way.

Examples are Important

> "There is one set of rules for managers and a different set of rules for staff. 99% of the organizations in the world work that way. There have to be different rules. Managers in this organization have a discretion to go early if they want, or not come back to work after a case, or go off to lunch. Staff don't. It has to be that way".

Wow...how about that for a quote! It was spoken by an assistant manager after a member of staff complained that managers seemed to have a life of ease and put in little hours compared to general employees. I found myself rooted to the floor as these words flowed from his mouth, caught in the center of that awful triangle that has shock, horror, and disbelief, as its corners. There are two hugely powerful words in the world of management: *Trust* and *Communication*. Not enough of either – and too much, or the wrong type, of communication – is the penalty we pay for setting bad examples. Incidentally, research has shown that error-based training can lead to greater improvements in training, i.e. showing how others made mistakes and how those mistakes can be

---

[166] As Mintzberg (2004) very aptly points out: Managers usually go away to programs alone, so they come back feeling isolated. They have learned new things and wish to make changes. But no one seems to care. P. 264.

[167] Leadership is often defined as "intentional influence". You will remember earlier references to "control" and "influence".

avoided seems to stick better with trainees.[168] Hence the quote above.

Over the years I have come to notice the huge volume of business and management books that highlight brilliant leaders with entire organizations following them down the road to glory. What is rarely mentioned, however, is the fact that *every* employee sets an example: many simply set *bad* ones.

There are two words here that I feel deserve special attention. First, the word *every*. I am always amazed when talking to people how many of them think example is something you lead by. This quite simply is not true. It does not just refer to the leaders at the top or even the managers throughout the entire organization: it refers to every person working there. All of our behaviors and words constitute the norms of organizational life around us. Second, the word *Bad*. It is an unhelpful word here. Instead we should say *unsuitable*. People are not bad. Using the word *bad* acts as a bar to generating commitment, buy-in, to building trust, so we will discard it and move on.

In order to highlight the importance of example setting, we should take a brief look at an experiment that became known as The Bobo Doll studies.[169] These studies demonstrated that children would become aggressive toward a doll after observing adults previously behaving in a similar fashion. In other words it is perfectly natural for children to imitate: it is how they learn and develop. And here's the kicker: adults do not lose this quality. Example is a very powerful role model and teacher.[170] So, you cannot expect to create a suitable manager or a suitable employee unless that individual had, in turn, the guidance and example of a suitable manager to follow.[171] Take it back to your home life. You

---

[168] Goldstein, Martin, and Cialdini (2007).
[169] Bandura et al. 1961, 1963.
[170] Adair (1983).
[171] Armstrong (2004).

cannot expect to raise a child properly suited to making a valuable contribution to society and family unless you set the child suitable guidance and examples.

> Parental example and modelling also has an impact on the development of self-esteem, a greater impact than the verbal advice parents give their children. Parents who cope with life challenges by using an active problem-solving coping style are more likely, [through their example], to help their children develop high self-esteem.[172]

Hurting the Ones We Love

The tragic reality of organizational life is that when a manager sets an unsuitable and damaging example it is the most diligent and conscientious workers who suffer more than the average worker. They feel a sense of hurt greater than anyone else simply because their hearts and minds are tied up in the success and vision of the organization. Negative occurrences, and negative interactions with others, have a bigger impact upon mood than positive occurrences or positive interactions. This should immediately send up a red flag for us. It indicates that setting a suitable example but then setting an unsuitable example afterwards sees us involved in a game of one step forward two steps back.

> It takes numerous encounters with positive people to offset the energy and happiness sapped by a single episode with one asshole.[173]

Conceptualizing the Issue

There is the danger – not helped by all those books out there on Leadership – that setting examples is viewed as flowing in one direction. As we are starting to see, however, everything everyone

---

[172] Carr (2004) p. 205. Square brackets added here for emphasis.
[173] Sutton (2007) P. 28.

does affects everyone around them (the Five Constituencies) no matter what level others are on. So, people might mistakenly believe that the following diagram represents the way in which example setting flows:

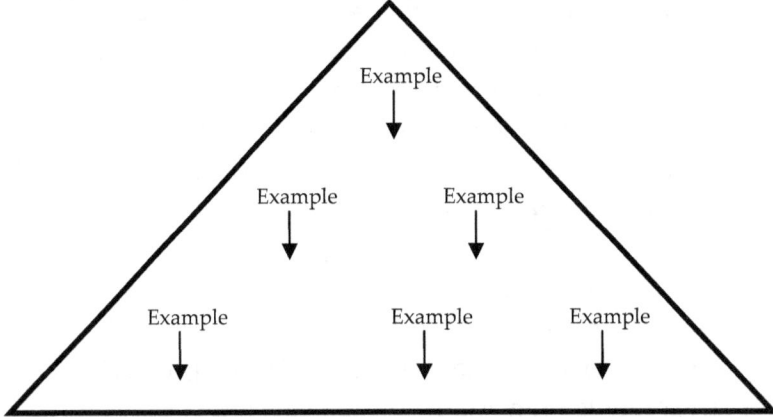

Note that Example here can represent suitable or unsuitable. The reality, however, is shown more clearly in the following diagram:

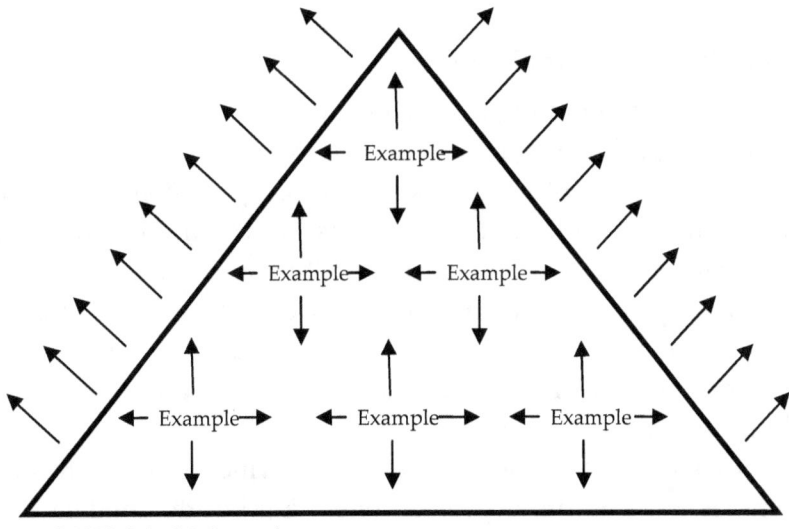

© 2008 Colm McCormack

Note the difference. Suitable or unsuitable, the reality is that example setting spreads out in all directions. This is crucial to both recognize and understand. Too many managers believe they only set examples when *deliberately* doing something, seemingly oblivious to the very real fact that everything they do everyday is spreading out like ripples on a pond. Note also the arrows pointing out from the organization itself. This is to take account of the External Stakeholders aspect of the Five Constituencies. So, we can say that example setting, whether suitable or unsuitable, radiates inward and outward to impact upon:

- ➤ The person setting the example him/herself (1st Constituency);
- ➤ The people around that person (2nd Constituency);
- ➤ The organization as a whole (3rd Constituency);
- ➤ External stakeholders, i.e. customers, business partners, suppliers, distributors, etc. (4th Constituency);
- ➤ You, the manager (5th Constituency).

Facts That Work Against Us

It is worth pointing out two simple facts of life that so many people caught up in organizational nonsense tend to overlook. First, the majority of our working day is spent going to, at, and coming from, work. But the effects of continuous unsuitable examples and the resulting harmful culture and climate extend our working day far beyond the work place. The negative impact of unsuitable behavior stretches out to touch our personal and home lives and manifests itself in the form of stress, arguments with our significant others – and more.

Second, if you sustain a culture in which setting unsuitable examples is the norm, if you say one thing but do another, and if the people you are trying to fool are the conscientious workers who suffer the most as a result of this type of behavior, you need to recognize the reality of the situation you have placed yourself in. Their eyes process up to 20 images per second,[174] their brains are running at 700-900 words per minute, but *you* can only bullshit at 200-400 words per minute. So, more than 50% of what is going on in their heads as you bullshit is not the words they are hearing! You have pitted yourself against very efficient and prolific processing machines. And everyday managers all around the world unleash these machines against themselves rather than for the benefit of their companies. It certainly points toward a total failure to understand people – an inability to manage.

But it gets worse. Too many business owners miss a very important point: customers can have significant impact upon your organizational culture – the way you do things. By scrambling to meet a customers needs, or re-jigging systems, processes, and procedures to win a new client, you are in fact messing around with your organizational culture. This may seem fine until you encounter a troublesome and potentially unprofitable customer. Seeking to satisfy such people can actually see you setting an unsuitable example. Generally, you need to drop these customers and move on. Bending things to fit *them* can see you warp the culture against yourself.

And then to top all this off we have the phenomenon that is the power of Blogs. These give people the power to reach out and hurt you if dissatisfied with the example you have set – the way in which you do business, the way you treat them, the lack of quality they feel they received. The simple fact that sites with the ending "sucks", i.e. your company name with the ending sucks dot com after it, came into existence should settle this point for you.

---

[174] Disputes among experts can see this figure range from 4-20 images per second with frames per second constituting a different topic.

Sink or Swim Time

> The illiterate of the 21st century will not be those who cannot read and write, but those who cannot learn, unlearn, and relearn.[175]

The time has arrived to break the cycle of unsuitable example setting and the ineffective organizational cultures that arise as a result. One of the key points to bear in mind is that humans, in general, respond in kind. It works perfectly well in the negative – set unsuitable examples and the culture goes to hell in a hand basket – so it works well too in the positive. Start setting suitable examples and people will start to get onboard the bus.

As we have seen throughout this book the simple truth is that if you always do what you've always done, you will always get what you always got. Bad situations do not deserve despair: they deserve managing. Take the answer that was given to me by a Team Leader in an insurance company. When I mentioned that the time had come to clean things up, to get management on the right track, to get them to work, take responsibility, turn up to work and make a worthwhile contribution, his reply was:

> "That would be like turkeys voting for Christmas. If you destroy the easy life they are having now then it won't be there for *you* when *you* are promoted to manager".

You can see how deeply ingrained the problem had become at that company. If that mindset goes unchallenged - if its affects go unmanaged - then that company will always get what it always got.

---

[175] Alvin Toffler, *The Third Wave*. Source: Templar (2006).

Look IN for the Solution Not Out

The starting point is for you to start setting suitable examples yourself. Sometimes there is just no hope of getting people to move until someone stands up and starts walking. On this point, I am reminded of a very pertinent quotation I came across along my travels:

> The way you live your life is as powerful a teaching for others as what you say to them.[176]

> Be the change that you wish to see in the world.[177]

Chapter 1 was you starting with yourself. Taking control of your personal life makes changing your own behavior at work so much easier. You then have to show everyone that they do indeed set an example in everything they say and do and these examples spread out to touch the four constituencies around them. You can start this process by working on your immediate team. Gerry Robinson provides some good advice in this regard:

> Your first responsibility is to get it right with your own team – those senior staff who report directly to you. It is vital to get this level operating well, so you should spend a significant amount of time examining the way they work, the quality of their work and the way they relate to other people. You should spend as much time on a one-to-one basis with them as you can so that you really get to know them…Trust and faith are so fundamental to all business relationships that if you have an uneasy feeling about somebody working for you, keep probing until you are either satisfied or you have asked them to move on. To ignore those underlying feelings will, I promise you, cost you dearly in terms of the success of the business.[178]

---

[176] Tom Cowan, shamanic practitioner, quoted by Templar (2005) pg. 178
[177] Gandhi.
[178] Robinson (2004) pg. 73

Having started with yourself as the center of the Five Constituencies, and then moved to your immediate team (people around you), you now turn to the general workforce of the business and then to the external stakeholders. People throughout the organization need to learn *how* they set an example and how they can improve upon the example they set for others. Remember, most people are unaware of even the most obvious forms of behavior simply because their focus is on fire-fighting, deadlines, etc. They need to know that even the examples they consider invisible and inaudible can still cause a ripple effect that others pick up on.

Your motivation for embarking upon this exercise is to be found in the old work maxim which states the better your team performs the better *you* look.[179] What we are now starting to see emerge is the idea of dealing with short-term problems – unsuitable example setting – by taking a long-term focus. By dealing with employees up close and personal, your organizational-wide aim of creating an effective culture - by stamping out the problem of unsuitable example setting - starts to take on meaning. Again, I will turn to Robert Sutton who states:

> Effective...management happens when there is a virtuous, self-reinforcing cycle between the 'big' things that organizations do and the little things that happen when people talk to one another and work together.[180]

The ultimate long-term positive effect of embarking upon this route is that you become an employer of choice – that Holy Grail or

---

[179] Previously, there was the fear-based belief that having great team members performing at their best constituted a threat to their manager since any one of them could be promoted to his job. This is still perfectly true today except there is now a corollary to the rule: yes they will be promoted to your job since you developed them but only after you have been promoted to another position (or rewarded in some equally meaningful way) in recognition of your manager-developing skills. The second corollary, of course, is that a failure to develop others should see you removed from your position.
[180] Sutton (2007) Pg. 81

state of enlightenment sought by so many HRM gurus. You make your own workers happier, the organizational culture more effective, and draw people to the company as your reward.

Spread Positivity like Wildfire – the P.S.C. Phenomenon

It is important at this point that we introduce the idea of *Social Contagion*. I propose defining this term as it will be used here as follows:

> The breakdown of organizationally enforced behavioral inhibitions in one person resulting in others following suit.

Imagine for a moment a company in which debate, playing devil's advocate, etc, is frowned upon. Then one day, during a manager's speech or pronouncement, someone suddenly raises a concern. That person has acted against the organizationally enforced behavioral inhibition which states *Thou shall not ask questions, disagree, or step out of line*. Others watching this may think, yeah, me too – and *there* is the contagious effect of the inhibition-breaking. The winning of hearts and minds leading to positive and suitable example setting is what we are looking for – what I refer to as *Positive* Social Contagion (PSC). The breaking of enforced inhibitions that simply lead to unsuitable example setting that spreads fear, dissatisfaction, apathy, etc - will be referred to as *Negative* Social Contagion (NSC). So people can break from enforced modes of behavior: the trick is to get them to break in the right direction.

An excellent example of this can be seen from the Gemini Project.[181] This was an I.T. change project (1996-2002) which aimed

---

[181] Ranganatham, C., Watson-Manheim, M.B., Keeler, J: *Bringing Professionals On Board: Lessons on Executing IT-Enabled Organizational Transformation*. MIS quarterly Executive Vol. 3 No. 3/September 2004.

to centralize 28 clinics into one state-of-the-art clinical facility in Illinois. There was widespread resistance to the change. Consultants and physicians did not see I.T. as part of their job. They saw it as an intrusion into the practice of medicine, felt they already had too much to do without inputting data into computers, and did not like the idea of their jobs becoming transparent. The excellent example, however, was set by the nurses. They were not I.T. literate at the start of the project. In the clinical chain of command, they had been relegated to nobodies by consultants and physicians. But the project was rolled out slowly using the nurses. They assessed their own jobs, gave presentations to senior management, and then started using the parts of the system that were rolled out to them. As a result, others in the clinics started noticing the nurses' jobs becoming easier. In time the, "How did you do that?" questions started coming from consultants and physicians. And here, for me, was the emergence of the positive social contagion. The nurses were smashing the organizationally enforced social inhibitions. In other words, they started using the I.T. system others considered taboo. By doing a lot of hard work, toughing out the resistance, unpleasantness, and hostility, the nurses set an example that eventually led to everyone – including those *above* them in the chain of command – following them.

The Co-Activity Syndrome

Watching football, basketball, and soccer, sees us watching sports in which the members of the teams depend on each other for success. This is known as *interacting*. It has been my experience, however, that the majority of companies I have come across are indulged in an alternative behavior that is *co-activity*: members of a department working alone on similar jobs, highly independent of others around them, and with little evidence of dependency on or coordination with each other.

Let's think about this for a minute. People doing the same kind of work in the one department. Yet, they don't depend on their work colleagues and don't need to engage in any coordination to get the job done. There is certainly nothing wrong with people capable of working on their own initiative. In fact, it is a quality of organizational life and recruitment campaigns that is highlighted quite strongly. But the focus on initiative over the years has led to the destruction of synergies. Take a look at the following all too familiar example of co-activity:

> ...in fully staffed medical units, it's natural to assume that multiple 'professional intelligences' (doctors, nurses, pharmacists) are working together to ensure that the best decisions are made, but under closer scrutiny only one of those intelligences may be functioning.[182]

Take a look at the diagram below:

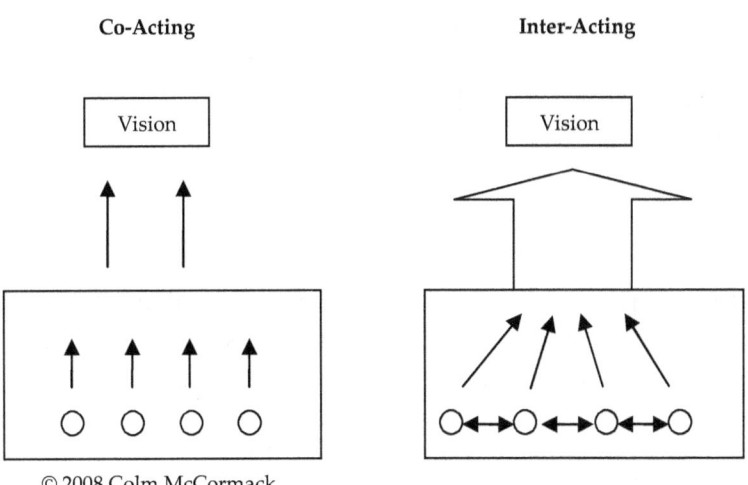

© 2008 Colm McCormack

The first part shows people simply co-acting – all doing their own thing. The second part shows an organization in which people

---

[182] Goldstein, Martin, Cialdini (2007) p. 90

are inter-acting. Note the synergies between the people and how they combine to produce greater driving force, efficiency and productivity.

The truth of course is that a lot of companies wander into a position of co-acting without realizing what is happening. Many of us have heard managers and supervisors say things like, "Come and go as you like so long as you get your work done". Such utterances seem to beg a culture of co- rather than inter-acting. We already have enough problems with departments not communicating or working with each other without discovering that within the individual departments themselves the situation is not much better - within the silos we now have islands! With inter-acting, however, we see vital synergies producing a greater overall organizational drive toward vision, operational and strategic goals.

This is not to say that the climate within such organizations is poor. It simply indicates that the culture is not as effective as it might be. We can immediately see a failure to leverage potential synergies that could exist if there was a greater level of interacting. Perhaps the best way to discuss this problem is to give an example of where it was overcome and the benefits that flowed from such a change.

Mobil North America Marketing and Refining introduced the Balanced Scorecard method of strategy management in the 1990s.[183] Up to that point – like most companies – co-activity would have been the norm on the ground. But as the scorecard measures and linkages were explained to the employees, things started to change. Truck drivers, after making a delivery to a gas station, started calling base to tell them they had noticed something not quite up to scratch that would lead to a mystery shopper flunking that particular station. This in turn would damage the *delight the customer* aspect of Mobil's strategy.

---

[183] Kaplan & Norton (2001).

We can immediately see two things happening here. First, the truck drivers are setting suitable examples. And they're not doing this from the top of the organization either. Second, we can see the element of interactivity emerging. Instead of simply driving their trucks, making deliveries and not worrying about anything else (co-acting), they are now doing things that will enable everyone in the organization strive for success. They are starting to *interact*.[184]

For the rest of us, however, there is the very real possibility that interacting is something that only occurs at the most basic of levels. In truth, a lot of us go to work and leave later that evening without having had too much need to rely on or assist others to any great extent. Recently, while passing Oscar Wilde's house on Merrion Square in Dublin, I saw an advert on a Dublin bus shelter for KPMG – the giant accountancy practice. There was a picture of a partner with a quote stating:

> You're only as good as the team around you. So it's great to work with the best.

But the implied promise of actually being the best is only true if each best individual is interacting with the other best individuals around him or her. If they are simply co-acting, then we have lots of the best people failing to maximize upon the potential synergies that come from properly linking and working with those around them.

In fact, our performance evaluation, incentive, and remuneration systems generally send silent cues that we co-act rather than inter-act. When I was working on a consultancy project at a top five law firm in Dublin, this problem seemed to present itself. I was aware of the general strategy within law firms that

---

[184] Please be careful, however. The Balanced Scorecard is simply what it says: score keeping. It should not be used as a panacea for bad management and the people subjected to it should not be managed by people incapable of managing themselves.

advocated cross-selling. My problem, however, was three-fold. First, nobody seemed to have measured the success, or otherwise, of cross-selling. How much additional revenues actually came from it? Second, what were the costs of cross-selling? Might a department or practice area – for example, the Property department – be kept open to serve the cross-selling strategy despite that department being the weakest in the firm's portfolio of expertise? And third, the real problem for me was the incentive system. Remember, lawyers are generally paid in terms of the hours they bill. And here's the problem. If I have a client and bill twenty hours on his sheet in a litigation matter, I might discover he wants to make a Will and sell some property. Cross-selling immediately tells me to send him to our Probate and Property departments. But I only get billed when *I* deal with him. Now others get to raise *their* billing hours, meet *their* targets, and benefit the firm as a whole. But it does not benefit me. In fact, I might even go so far as to state I am *punished* for sending him across the hall because others rack up their billing hours for the privilege without any form of kick-back to me. Others are helped in their race to become Partner at the firm before I do. In other words, a lot of law firms have members interacting at the very surface, but deep down their incentive systems perpetuate the reality: co-acting.

The Reality Factor

I constantly advocate that there is no such thing as a one-fits-all model in business. And it is a warning we must be aware of here. One of the first questions I always encourage managers to ask themselves is this: why bother? We have been talking here about setting a good example, starting with you, and getting others to follow through positive social contagion. But we must ask the question of whether or not, in our own organizations, we should go to the bother of doing this.

One of the awful realities of organizational life is that nothing breeds failure quite like success. The choice of not fixing what does not appear to be broken is a dangerous one. Doing nothing sees companies entertaining short-term success without any long-term focus. Successful times are the best for making effective changes. You have the luxury of time, consideration. When bad times arrive, however, organizations find themselves too slow and stodgy to react, too full of people programmed with the wrong mindsets. Change is forced upon them. Plans are poorly thought-out and proactivity is replaced by reactivity.

Therefore, the principle of suitable example setting is ultimately a choice for you to make, but one I would urge you to make for the long-term benefit of the business, your own sanity, and the happiness of those who work with you.

Your Physical Behaviors

Is is important that you start to consider idea of starting with yourself before rushing out to influence other people. Consider the small subtle things you can do over a significant period of time that might make things easier for you in the long-term:

> Practice self-observation as you talk with people.[185]
>   o Do you fiddle with your hands or objects close to hand?
>   o Do you shift your weight from foot to foot?

---

[185] Self-monitoring serves as a catalyst for change (Wilson, 1998). It is a fundamental part of improved self-regulation (Bandura, 1986). Knowing the connections between your behavior and the factors that influence that behavior can enable you to perceive ways of becoming more effective (Hawton et al, 2006).

- Do you make regular and sustained eye contact?
- Do you give the clear impression you are listening?
- Do you stop what you're doing and give them your full attention?

So we've moved from the mental and attitudinal to the physical impact of our behavior. I have always found this fascinating when observing and coaching executives and managers; you'd be amazed at the little yet distracting quirks they engage in when talking to those around them.

More importantly, your physical actions and behaviors are a two-way street: they are often a manifestation of what is going on in your mind but they are also a method for changing internal mood and thinking. For example, we might expect a defensive or threatned person to sit with their arms crossed, looking stern - the physical behaviour manifested by the internal defensive thinking or feeling. However, getting such a person to change their physical position can lead to their internal feelings or thinking changing too – the two-way street effect. Observing, leading, and managing the people around you is more fully a topic for discussion in book two of this series, yet worth noting here in terms of managing ourselves.

Some Final Thoughts

> No longer talk at all about the kind of man that a good man ought to be, but be such.[186]
> Be the change that you wish to see in the world.[187]

The best any of us can do is start with ourselves and then make a determined effort to start practicing these principles at

---

[186] Marcus Aurelius. X, 16, p. 87.
[187] Gandhi.

home. When you openly talk about goals, about being fair, about your dislike of gossip, your children will come to view suitable example setting as natural. If we get it right at home we can get it right at work. We move from ourselves, to our families, to our immediate working team, to the rest of the organization, to our stakeholders. This will have a powerful spill-over effect on both fronts. Too many colleges and books tell us to set a truly inspiring vision and then people will follow us. The truth, however, is that people have to buy into the would-be leader first. Then, when they're happy with that they'll chase the vision.

Setting suitable examples, when carried out honestly and not as a device for deception, is an indication the person can manage themselves. It heralds the coming of managerial maturity since there is a move away from preaching to actually doing what is preached – from being able to state what is good management in academic terms to actually carrying it out themselves and not sitting idly-by forcing others to do it instead. When we set suitable examples from a base of strong, informed, and reflective self-management, we are beaming outward to the world the message that we are fit to lead and manager others.

Chapter 10
"Leader, Leader, Leader" –

Chanting the Wrong Mantra?

Leaders

I sometimes find myself at the center of a storm when I tell people that life is all about management and nothing more. "But what about *leaders*?" is the question that follows immediately. And let me be crystal-clear here: leaderSHIP – yes; leadER – not so much.

So, what exactly does a leadER do according to all the experts out there? We are told he or she sets the vision for us. They get us to move toward it. They inspire us. They generate buy-in, commitment and trust. But the actual truth is that he or she *manages* the vision of an organization, *manages* your perception of them as individuals, *manages* their own behavior and the way he or she expresses attitudes and opinions. For me, leadership is simply management of higher level things: everything in life comes back to management. And this is important for you too: placing a person on a pedestal gives them little choice but to look down on you; it also prevents you yourself from stepping up to the mark if you, for some reason, view yourself as not having been ordained 'leadER' by the organization.

The focus of the business world has been totally hijacked in recent years by academics focusing on Leadership. Its place on many business college curricula is muscling out time usually devoted to other topics. Everyone wants to be a Bill Clinton, a Jack Welch, a Steve Jobs, an Obama.

Those managers who cannot lead are simply ineffective managers. Those who *can* lead are effective managers, not leadERs - creatures of a different name. So, leadership is a quality we would expect a good manager to have. Having it should see us elevate him within an organization but not to an iconic position in business folklore – the 'LeadER'. Would we all rush out to study courses and read books that would turn us into "Decision-ers", "Meeting-ers", "Agenda-ers" "Spreadsheet-ers"? Would we all hail people with these titles and pay them insane amounts of money? Yet when we display the management quality of leading, we become "leaders" and are often grossly over-paid for it.

More to the point, to say that a company must have excellent leadership and a fantastic culture to survive is a total nonsense. Having these things is simply nice, an added bonus. I have encountered many companies devoid of any leadership and with climates so bad that people would shoot each other quicker than utter a civil word. Yet the companies were incredibly successful and continue to be.[188] I am one of the biggest advocates of suitable organizational culture and climate[189] you could ever hope to meet,

---

[188] Granted, they could probably be even more successful if the types of leadership and organizational culture that books talk about were put in place. But the point must be clear: you can make money and profit without such concepts.

[189] In simple terms, "culture" is a history of shared learning and the way things are done in an organization as a result, e.g. bureaucratically, or openly and free-thinking with everyone getting involved, etc. "Climate" refers more to the prevailing atmosphere, e.g. friendly, war-zone like, vicious, etc. Generally there will be an overall organizational culture but there can

but I have to recognize that companies have been in existence for decades before these topics ever became fashionable and many continue to exist while totally ignoring such ideas. You should recognize this too.

Leader versus Manager

The qualities that make a good leader have intrigued psychologists, politicians and historians for years: nobody knows what the exact qualities are or should be.[190] There are countless definitions out there, as if seeking to reinforce the sense of bewilderment on the topic. The most common feature of most of the definitions, however, is that of *influence*. Leaders are usually viewed as exerting influence over others in order to get things done. But so too are managers. The most common point of focus when dealing with leadership is that of *effectiveness* – just how *effective* a particular person is as a leader. Same when looking at you in your role as manager: are you effective or not? There seems little to suggest we should carve out a new creation and set it apart from that of the manager.

Intentionally influencing people should not seem strange to you at this stage. Using the power of positive social contagion, setting suitable examples, using positive consistency and interacting with others are all elements of the overall managerial skill set that have become familiar to you. Observation will allow you decide how and when to use such influencing tactics.

Academics, as we know, like to separate management from leadership. You should see the expressions on the faces every

---

also be sub-cultures. So, for example, it may be friendly and free-spirited in the marketing department but regimented, silent and cold in the accounting department, and so on.
[190] Aronson et al (2004).

semester when I list off the supposedly leader versus managerial areas of focus. Take a look at the list for yourself:

A Leader:	A Manager:
Innovates	Administers
Develops and Focuses on people	Focuses on systems
Inspires trust	Controls
Looks to the future	Watches the bottom line

In the real world, however, you must recognize that most of this stuff goes hand-in-hand and is embodied within the same person. If we review the leadership literature covered by business students, we can say that:

- Leadership is an **influence** process, therefore
- Leadership involves the use of **politics** since
- Leadership is a **leveraging** activity suggesting
- Leadership is not a **lone warrior** activity.

Put another way, dodging uncomfortable organizational politics, sitting in your comfort zone and going it alone to take all the glory is much the same as turning up at the starting line for the marathon with both ankles bound together; any leader adopting this *modus operandi* will not get very far. But are all these things not present in the world of management too? As a manager you will have to influence, get into the politics of it all, leverage what you can, get involved with others and work outside your comfort zone. The higher up the management ladder you go, the more these things occur. So at what point do you attract the "leader" label?

The Management Skill Set Model

The entire point of looking at the manager versus leader issue here is to help you avoid falling into a mindset whereby you do nothing until you get to the top position within your organization or you start to see leaders as radically different people from yourself. Don't fall for that kind of nonsense thinking. You can get moving *now* and make positive things happen irrespective of whether you hold a high ranking position and the power that goes with it.[191]

For the purposes of our discussion, let us construct a model and see how this helps our understanding of the topic. First, let us represent an average executive and look at the skill set he draws upon to retain his position within the organization.

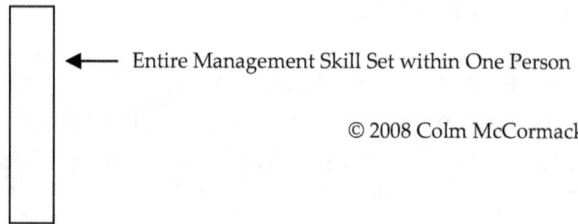

Entire Management Skill Set within One Person

© 2008 Colm McCormack

What we are looking at here is his entire skill set hence one entire rectangle. Let us now continue our working hypothesis which states that everything he does is management. In order to deal with leadership, it is portrayed in our model as a trait or quality or skill contained within the executive's overall skill set. In order for us to view it, we must therefore break the leadership skills out from the overall management skills. That enables us to now look at his overall skill set as follows:

---

[191] There are of course several forms of power of which "positional" power is just one.

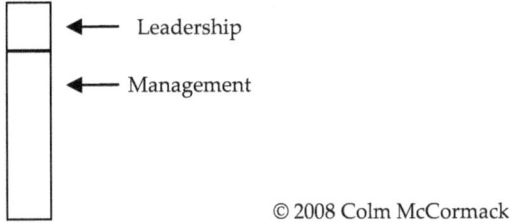

Now we see management and leadership as two different elements within the overall management skill set. Already at this point some would have us believe it is a totally different person. But it's simply the same person using a particular aspect of his overall skill set. Let us assume that the above skill set picture indicates 90% management skills and 10% leadership skills. For notation purposes, this is represented as: 90M:10L. We shall refer to this as his Capacity. His management capacity is 90, or 90M, and his leadership capacity is 10, or 10L.

Now we must allow for reality in our model. In everyday life, we know that an athlete, for example, will not always be at the top of his game. He may require further training, an altered diet, years of dedication. So he is aiming to reach his full potential. Potential in the sporting world equates to Capacity in our model. Until he reaches his full potential (Capacity) he is only ever at any given level of Fitness. Now let us view this in our model:

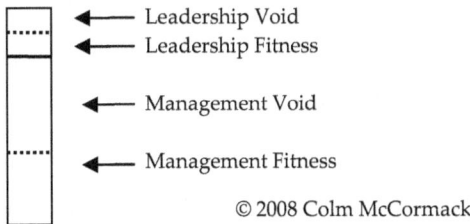

Here we see the executive's Capacity of 90M:10L, but we also see his Fitness 40/90M:2/10L. When we have an indication of Fitness, and both Management and Leadership Capacities, then we know his Effective Skill set. In other words, this particular executive can greatly enhance his overall management skills. He has sufficient Capacity for improvement. In athletic terms, he has the potential to run the marathon in two and a half hours but is currently only fit enough to run it in four. Therefore, our model now shows Capacity, Fitness and Void (the area for improvement between Fitness and Capacity). There are many ways to look at how we can write and view this in notation terms:

- Skill Set = M Capacity + L Capacity

- Effective Skill Set = (M Capacity – M Fitness) + (L Capacity – L Fitness)

- Fitness = Capacity – Void

- Capacity = Fitness + Void

- Void = Capacity - Fitness

It is at this point that we start to see the famous Peter Principle emerge. It states that eventually everyone is promoted to the level of their own incompetence. In simple terms, I will be promoted higher and higher until I get to a level at which I cannot cope. This would tell the person promoting me that I should have stayed at the level prior to the latest promotion. Our model allows for this. Any position requiring a high level of leadership Capacity and Fitness should not see a person with the 40/90M:2/10L Effective skill set promoted to that position.

Our Three Labels

Capacity in our model can never be set at zero. The fact that a person gets out of bed in the morning, showers, eats breakfast and travels to work indicates an ability to manage. If this is as far as their management skills go, fine. At worst they will have a 1M:xL notation assigned to them. Leadership is the same. At worst, a parent will demonstrate even menial leadership abilities on occasion when dealing with their children. So, at worst they will have an xM:1L notation assigned to them, or an overall permitted minimum skill set of 1M:1L.

Fitness is also easy to understand. The crucial point, however, is that Fitness can never exceed Capacity. Again this makes sense. In theory, an athlete may never reach his full potential. A world record holder may consider himself at the peak of his career but his Capacity may actually be higher. Training methods and specialized diets, undiscovered at the time the athlete was competing, will come along to reveal that he may have actually run faster than his *declared* fastest. In other words, the current state of technology limited his Fitness such that he never reached his true Capacity.[192] This reveals two things in our model. First, we can never know what our true Capacity is – we can only make a reasonably accurate estimation, and second, not only will our Fitness never surpass our Capacity, it will never equal it or stay close to it for long. In the case of our executive, he will become subject to experience, habit, rule-of-thumb decision making, all of which will limit his Fitness and prevent him knowing his true Capacity. In the executive's world, success can actually lead to him increasing his Void, as one-fits-all ways of thinking and pro-longed exposure to similar experiences prevent him reaching higher levels of Fitness. A person with high

---

[192] Note that Michael Phelps record 8 Olympic gold medals in 2008 saw him, in some cases, beating Mark Spitz's world records by ten seconds! Might Spitz have been greater had he been born into the same generation as Phelps or might Phelps have been worse if born into Spitz's generation?

capacity but very low Fitness should exhibit an almost extraordinary initial rate of progress when adequate training and development is provided to them. A person with significant Capacity will not have a slowing of the rate of increase in Fitness until that Fitness starts to close in on Capacity.

Our third label is that of the Void. This is the difference between our Fitness and our Capacity. It is crucial to recognize that a Void may grow as well as shrink. If we fail to train, indulge in self-improvement, have too narrow an experience range, then our overall Fitness falls and the Void grows.

What Might it all Mean?

There is a natural tendency to assume that a great leader has a huge leadership Capacity. We might assume they have a 50M:50L skill set makeup. Within that, we might further assume they have a 40/50M:45/50L Effective skill set. But this is where things in the real world, the world outside our model, start to go wrong. Think of former American president Bill Clinton, or Jack Welch or Henry Ford – any individual often referred to as "leader" in the leadership books. Let us assume that he decides to work an eight hour day. Four hours of this will be spent displaying excellent leadership ability giving speeches. To assign a 50M:50L skill set to him simply because that is how his *time* is spent, would be a huge error. There is a crucial distinction to be made between leadership Capacity and Fitness, and time spent displaying whatever level of Fitness actually exists within the person. What we might actually be witnessing is a 60/90M:8/10L skill set. All he is doing is spending 50% of his *time* demonstrating, to great effect, the 8% leadership within his overall management skill set. In other words, the 8% Fitness within his 10% leadership Capacity may be all he needs for what he is required to do but the huge amount of time spent doing it makes it look bigger than it really is.

How Should We Hire People?

From our model and ensuing discussion we see a crucial question that is never properly asked, let alone properly answered. "Is he or she a good manager?" may actually be the wrong question in the everyday world of business. Let me give you an example. Jane has never worked as a manager. Nor has she ever been to business school nor had any type of executive training. Therefore, the logical answer to our question is that she is not suitable for promotion to management. But that is because we have asked the wrong question. We should be asking what her management Capacity and Fitness are and what her Leadership Capacity and Fitness are. What if she has a 30/80M:18/20L effective skill set make up? Here we see someone who, with a little training, could be a fantastic manager. We also see that not only does she have leadership Capacity, her Fitness in that category is extremely high. In everyday parlance, she presents as a natural born leader. Asking the wrong question therefore means the generation of the right answer becomes impossible. Furthermore, the Age and Experience Trap section of this book will find an answer here or a partial answer: a seemingly young and inexperienced person may nonetheless have high Fitness and significant Capacity suited to the job for which they are being turned away (you will remember the giant drinks marketing company story earlier in Chapter 8).

There is the very real possibility that people with great potential are not being promoted. That's hardly a revelation to any of us. The flip side to this is that people with limited skills, but where those limited skills are sharp, are being promoted over others. In the language of our model, people with high Capacity are judged on their visible Fitness. That Fitness may be low compared to the Fitness level another person *could* achieve if only they received the proper training. Therefore, we may conclude that any organization hiring people on their visible Fitness alone, while ignoring their Capacity, is simply looking for a quick fix. The trend toward low cost in the business world has a case to answer here. The focus on visible costs of training employees, be they entry or executive level, blinds us to the long-term opportunity costs (or invisible costs) of foregoing the cost of training and taking people with lesser Fitness.

Another view we can take is the one we took while using Bill Clinton as an example. We are justified taking the low-cost route and foregoing training employees if the visible Fitness they exhibit suits perfectly the position to which we want to hire them. So, training everyone because books and gurus tell us to can be very wrong, depending upon the situation (training is therefore Context Sensitive). We simply want him to do the job we give him and which he is currently very good at. Again, however, this may be short-sighted of us. It assumes he will stay in that job, at that level, on that level of pay forever. If he becomes bored, or that particular job becomes unnecessary due to a change in organizational strategy, then our ability to move him to another position within the organization is limited. Potentially, the ability to promote from within disappears over time for an organization that takes this approach with all of its employees.

In the most basic of terms, our model suggests three initial and obvious courses of action open to us for three different kinds of people:

High Capacity but low Fitness	Train them
High Capacity and high Fitness	Consider Promotion and keep them sharp
Low Capacity	Limited training over time with very limited promotion only to positions very specifically suited to their Fitness

A lot of business schools churn out MBAs every year with fantastic leadership Fitness but recruitment can be questionable. So, if these MBAs do not get a high ranking job within a short period of time then problems start to emerge. Taking a low-level job runs not only the risk that the Fitness will recede and the Void grow, but they will get on their fellow workers nerves. This will happen if the menial tasks go undone because the MBA is exercising leadership skills in too superior a ratio to all the other skills in the overall management skill set.

Styles of Leadership and Management

Academia deals with leadership under headings such as trait approaches, behavioral approaches, situational approaches, transformational leadership, etc. Some people advocate getting the right man for the job. If times are hard, get a tough talking trouble shooter. If times are good, get a smooth suave guy who will charm the shareholders. Academics argue over whether trait or style approaches are better. So many different types of leaders. Why not just *manage* the situation instead? Why get complicated?

A manager who can manage himself should be able to switch between the various styles demanded by the times. Most of us do not have the luxury of switching managers whenever the times dictate. There are employment laws of varying strength in different countries around the world. It takes time to notice a shift in the external environment. It takes time and expense and upsets many apple carts ditching a manager and replacing and training a new one. Just think about what a lot of books out there are advocating: things change so get a different person with a different style of leadership. Oh yeah? Think time lag, cost, the effects on everyone around the old and new leader, the potential threat to the culture of your company, etc. You might switch lead-er, but what else might you inadvertently alter?

From Theory to Practice

You must resolve from now on not to sit around waiting to get to the top before making things better; example, behaviour, communication, attitude – even bullying!! - flow in all directions. Don't set out to become an anarchist or ruin your career. Consider how you might slowly and subtly make things better both at work and at home. Remember; time takes time.

Sit down with your HR Director and discuss your hiring policies. Hopefully, you will have already chatted with them on avoiding the Age & Experience Trap that was mentioned in Chapter 8. Explore how you might move toward hiring people with high Capacity for the positions you will need to fill in the future. Explore how you might test for candidates who have high levels of Fitness or are capable of increasing their fitness rapidly if nurtured.

Over time, it might be a good idea for both of you to revisit all existing job holders within the organization to determine if:

> ➢ The right choices were made;
> ➢ People with the right Capacity and Fitness are holding those positions;
> ➢ Some people require additional training;
> ➢ Anybody is being passed over for promotion due to the wrong policies/standards remaining in place.

Decide whether or not Context affords you the time to hire for the long view and create a wealth of talent capable of moving from position to position if/when required. Again – Context Sensitive mixed with Constantly Reassess; there's no point talking about these concepts if you do not put them into practice within the organization as a managerial default setting – move from theory to on-the-ground practice. This will be your effective management with true leadership quality potential built in.

Some Final Thoughts

It is far too easy to arrive at the mistaken assumption that becoming successful and effective is simply a matter of studying leadership. The bookshelves are stacked with titles that give off this impression and they're being read by time-pressed individuals seeking the ultimate quick fix. But these books are simply teaching management. Has the word *management* become so unpalatable that we must now teach it through the side door – under a different heading?

So where is all this going? Are we out to row back decades of research and millennia of the word *leader*? No, not at all. But what you must do is maintain Constantly Reassess on high alert for this subject. What we are trying to do is apply the brakes on a run away topic that has the potential, if left unchecked, to cause some serious damage. Just how pertinent is the idea of leadership and a leader in the every day lives of the average Joe or Jane? To suggest leadership is a vital aspect in the lives of the average person is nonsense. Remember, the over whelming majority of businesses out there are small privately held ones. We're living in a manager's world, populated by managers - a world craving real and effective management. And yet, at the same time, we're all trying to shed our skin to become something else. Academia would have us all in denial. Take it to its absurd conclusion: everybody being developed into leaders would see the world grind to a halt.[193] No one would

---

[193] This is why in Chapter 9 I said everybody *sets* an example rather than everybody *leads* by example.

know how – never mind want to – do the menial yet crucial tasks of every day societal and organizational life. A manager should be able to do a piece of everything; your job is to hire people smarter than you and then manage the experts; develop them into the effective managers of tomorrow. You starting place will be with YOU; develop and manage yourself first before attempting to develop, lead, and manage others.

Conclusion

Everything in this book applies whether or not you hold a position within the organizational managerial ranks. These are lessons for life – lessons you can and should apply for all time throughout your career.

The starting point – as this book demonstrates – is YOU! The topics covered in this first book enable you arrive into book two ready – fit and effective – to turn toward how you lead and manage others. This book sees you focusing on your Leadership Brand – on installing the foundations upon which to build your approach to leading and managing others. You wouldn't turn up at the starting line for a marathon having never run before! And yet, so many people within the managerial ranks of organziations have done precisely that in their careers: they were good at doing a particular thing so were promoted on that criteria alone into a position of control over people – and what a mess that makes!

We know that managers who cannot manage themselves cause distraction, unnecessary problems, damage to morale and organizational culture. They promote the use of fire-fighting bandaid-type mindsets to tackling symptoms rather than the actual cause. Often, their biggest obstacle is themselves. Very often, the symptoms they are tackling have emanated from their own behavior, psychology, perspective and attitudes.

The entire point behind this book was to reach back beyond where most other business and management books start to the person who is the manager. By doing so, we front-load our efforts thereby enabling us to kill a lot of problems before they even arise. At this point, it should now be clear to you that effective management has its benefits and is less hassle than ineffective management with all its fire-fighting and symptom-tackling demands and constraints. It should also be clear to you that management is not just something that occurs in the office: *living is managing* – everything we do requires some level of management. The absurdity of emerging from chaos, managing at work, and then returning home to chaos is something you are now alert to.

We know that managers derail for the same reasons. They fall down on issues of emotional stability, defensiveness and interpersonal skills. To these we added locus of control, context ignorance, unsuitable example setting, ego, blame, a failure to reframe, negativity and negative people, and more. This entire book has moved you through a process of avoiding these pitfalls by learning the reasons managers derail, reflecting upon your own behavior, observing others, building ego strength, and moving you toward making Constantly Reassess one of your dominant habits to push you toward becoming Context Intelligent. Along this road, we were mindful that a change in any one of the following: thought, mood, behavior, physical reaction or our environment, can effect the other four, i.e. a change in one can see benefits for all five of these factors. In our personal lives, this helps us to avoid what I refer to as the "Human Default Life Plan" – born, go to school, get a job, get married, have kids, retire, see what happens - and enables us to determine when we have started to focus on the wrong social reference group. On the professional front, we saw that goals in both our personal and professional lives should be managed on an overall basis without one set overshadowing the other. The entire process was underpinned by the BabySteps concept with the Fat Friday method affording us a comforting safety net.

Managers need to watch, listen, and interpret. Our observation is improved through the use of the Five Constituency Model for Observing Behavioral Impact. This is *not* a paralysis-by-analysis model. It is designed to get you to pause only briefly and look beyond yourself and the *obvious* implications of any behavior or decision thereby avoiding what I term the "False Reality" problem. It helps make you aware of Context, it aids in expanding the number of Choices you see before you. It encourages big picture thinking and helps you develop effective and targeted action that contains the impact of your actions from the other constituencies. The model works for both personal and professional settings, and can be inverted to place *you* at the center as viewed by another observer. There are ten positives – the Ten Ps - to this that can be rhymed off in the following process:

> **Pause** to consider **Position** and **Perspective** to **Prevent** you making the wrong choices thereby enabling you to adopt a **Positive**, well **Prepared**, and **Pro-active** approach to improve potential **Performance**, all of which represents **Positive consistency** and is something you should **Perpetuate** to the benefit of all Five Constituencies since it ensures that Action is dictated by Context and is regulated by Constantly Reassess.

The Five Constituency model, its associated Ten Ps, and the concept of Positive Consistency, enable us make the right Choices to lessen or improve the Demands made of us and reduce or improve the Constraints under which we operate. In this regard, I have expanded the idea of Demands emanating from the job description only and allowed it to cover unreasonable demands made by emotional employees and other factors that do not recognize simple boundaries such as duties, responsibilities, and job description.

These models and concepts also enable us prevent others from getting in our way or their own way by observing behavior in context. When others see us behaving in these positive ways we are said to be setting suitable examples. And this is important. Example setting spreads out in all directions from every person within the organization or family irrespective of position, rank, or title: it does not flow from the top down only. A failure to move from Negative to Positive Consistency will see you setting unsuitable examples for others and Warping the Psychological Contract thereby inviting blame to migrate to you.

In everything you do, the *Outer Rings* are farthest from your center of focus and can therefore have a nasty cumulative effect if devoid of Constantly Reassess. Under severe circumstances, a major breach in one aspect of your life can spread out to impact upon all areas. We saw this with the example of taking heroin in your personal life or committing serious fraud in your professional life: the impact from one will spread out to both professional and personal aspects of your life.

As a manager, you will be aware of three commonly unpopular topics within organizational life that require closer examination and reassessment: ego, politics, and conflict. None of these are bad despite what so many will tell you. It is not a case of leaving your ego at the door: you must not proceed beyond the door without sufficient *ego strength*. The entire process put forward by this book aims to develop ego strength by focusing on proactivity, internal locus of control, seeking feedback, considering the impact we have upon the Five Constituencies through our actions or inactions. We know that as you rise within an organization, political skill becomes essential. Far too many people have negative and destructive-type politics in mind whenever this topic is brought up. The same can be said of conflict and confrontation: both are essential. Conflict can be said to escalate until wellbeing is achieved or restored.

As a manager, your ability to learn from and about others is underpinned by Communication. Everything a person does or does not do communicates something. This is why learning, pausing, observing, assessing, reflecting, and effective listening have featured strongly in this book. Communication is not just about speaking and sending memos. It is about body language, posture, facial expression, silence, unintended communications, acting, not acting, and more. A manager must be able to know, understand, and manage his/her own communications repertoire in addition to being able to interpret the repertoires of those around them. The ability to listen effectively, to get behind the words to the true meaning of what is communicated, is a key skill. Often, your job will be to unearth a reason the other person may not even be aware of themselves. This is why I placed so much value on face-to-face communications. A failure to understand and interpret the communications repertoire of others, and to effectively listen, will simply see blame migrate to you when problems arise as a result of your failure to manage effectively.

From reaching back beyond where most books start to creating Context Intelligent Managers, all underpinned by the philosophy that to manage others effectively you must first be able to manage yourself: that has been my entire reason for writing this book. When you are aware of the context you have been in, are currently in, and are trying to create, then all actions and decisions are better informed. This is the front-loaded effort and the moving of quality to the start of the entire management process. Children assess context quite easily and naturally but they also withdraw when the context is unsuitable. As managers, however, we have a tendency to ignore context and bitch and moan about the expense, time and effort that demands we proceed in a *full speed ahead damn the torpedoes* misplaced mentality. The best strategy in the world is doomed if introduced into the wrong context. It is for such reasons that creating context intelligent managers must become a top priority for the business and management schools. Until it does, it is every manager's duty to strive for such a position under their own steam.

The key to Context Intelligence is Constantly Reassess. This is an inbuilt default setting that you must work to install as a strong and powerful habit in your psyche. Context can change. The right plan can suddenly be cast as ineffective if you are not reassessing context and the actions you are or are not taking. Asking yourself questions, reframing, using the Five Constituency model, observing others – everything – it's all Constantly Reassess: it's all taking you toward becoming Context Intelligent.

We all spend a great many hours each day travelling to, at, and travelling from work. What is left is our personal or home life. In those two simple spheres – work and personal – time is precious and scarce enough without failing to manage effectively. When we can manage ourselves we spread suitable examples out to those around us. If we can get enough people mimicking our positive consistency then we can move from co-acting to interacting. Our example teaches others to manage themselves without us expressly stating that our mission is to teach. Example setting reduces so much resistance and so many barriers. Example is powerful because it speaks for itself. Nobody has to announce it; it's just there. You don't have to be at the top of the organizational hierarchy with the *leader* tag hanging around your neck. Everything we have discussed doing in this book *is* fantastic leadership in action: you are observing, refusing to dive in before getting the facts, setting suitable examples, managing your communications repertoire, walking around to get the views of everyone you can, and more. It is all leadership according to so many books out there but *we* know it to be effective and suitable management. Our managerial skill sets contain the ability to manage higher order things – things others would refer to as leadership or leadership tasks.

The Wheel of Change

With this book I have brought you through the Wheel of Change. Hopefully, everything covered has been helping you toward change – in outlook, perspective, attitude, thinking, managing, and more. I have borrowed the Wheel of Change from the world of addiction counseling.[194]

We can use the wheel to say the following:

Phase 1:	Before picking up this book you may have been unaware of any need to change your behavior when looking at management.
Phase 2:	Reading the book, hopefully, caused you to realize that some personal adjustment was called for. You started to reassess.
Phase 3:	The ongoing discussions enabled you prepare for change.
Phase 4:	You started taking action toward change.
Phase 5:	You started adjusting to the idea of change and started practicing new skills to sustain change.
Phase 6:	Relapse. People suffering from addiction often relapse before reaching success. For our purposes, this is the Fat Friday method. There will be times when you relapse into your old style of management. Once Fat Friday has passed, you resume the cycle again. Failing here will not see blame migrate to you: it will see the more desirable and constructive Productive Blame attach instead.

Observing others allowed for error-based learning – watching others making the same mistakes over and over allowed you to reinforce the positives in yourself.

Any of us who have had to push a car or paddle a kayak know intuitively that it takes less energy to sustain motion than to continually re-start. We can say the same for addiction, habit breaking, and bringing about change: if you break the cycle through stopping or relapsing you have to put in a tremendous amount of

---

[194] Sourced from:
http://www.camh.net/About_Addiction_Mental_Health/Drug_and_Addiction_Information/Addiction_Information_Guide/addiction_change.html

energy to get going and build up momentum again. Therefore, observation, reflection – and all the other topics covered in this book – are ongoing: the entire process is a journey not a destination.

Simple Do's for Moving Forward

Don't surrender to the increasingly popular view that life these days is harder than ever before. That's total nonsense. Appreciation is what has become harder. Today, there seems to be an ever growing wave of willingness to find hardship, problems, despair. But as we saw earlier, it is up to you not to run with the crowd – to constantly reassess the conventional wisdom that now borders upon popular nonsense. Learning to manage yourself before taking on the task of managing others can see you move from existing to living, from creating problems to tackling them, from problem-oriented mindsets to solution-oriented.

- Set out a simple Life Plan on paper. Make sure the goals you have in life and at work are managed without one set overshadowing the other;[195]
- Ask. Always ask! Plug into the experience of others and access their wisdom. The two most powerful words in the English language are *ask* and *no*. It never ceases to amaze me just how many people are afraid to use both of them to make managing life and work so much easier;
- Enjoy *Now*. Move on from the past, plan for the future, but don't forget to enjoy life, your family, and your career today;
- Keep a Success Diary! This is not some touchy-feely hippy notion. Success diaries are a bit like networking and praying: nobody thinks about them until it's too late!

---

[195] Again, I highly recommend you visit www.briantracyinternational.com for guidance here.

- As a manager, you must see problems, failures, and rejection in a new light, in a different way – they are a part of life and, at times, you must actually seek them out if you are to break free of many organizational gravitational holds;
- Get away from negative people;[196]
- Stop complaining! Complainging – like gossip – is addictive and contagious. You want to adopt a solution-oriented mindset, govern your emotions, stay positive;
- Break everything down into little chunks: BabySteps;
- Pause. View each situation through the lens of the Five Constituency model to bring about the Ten Ps and Positive Consistency;
- Investigate first. Don't just dive into solving employee issues;
- Improve the Demands, Constraints, and Choices at work and at home;
- Delegate![197]
- Meet with your HR Director to discuss:
    - Job and portfolio rotation;
    - Your hiring criteria and policies – look beyond experience as a sole criteria;
    - Previous hiring and promotion decisions;
    - How to examine every job role within the organization to determine what is actually needed to perform each;
    - How to examine each persons skill set within the organization to determine if the right people are in the right jobs;
    - How to improve all of these things for the future;

---

[196] NOT people *bringing* you negative news or results – there's a world of difference.
[197] See book two in this series: The 'PEOPLE' Factor for discussion on when to delegate, what to delegate and to whom – plus the Five-Rs of delegation.

- How to encourage and champion healthy and constructive confrontation;
- Manage and deal with conflict. Ignoring it will not make it go away;
- Become aware of, and monitor, organizational politics;[198]
- Concentrate on developing your ego strength;
- Make sure the reasons you are hearing are in fact reasons and not excuses;
- Watch and measure the little things;
- Be consistent in mood, investigations, decision making, distributing awards and contracts. A lack of transparency will only serve to warp the psychological contract against you and the organization;
- Observe others to ensure:
  - You act when you should;
  - You act when you need to;
  - You get the full picture;
  - You see what is *really* going on;
  - You can head off trouble before it arises;
  - You know who is on who's side;
  - You know what you are actually up against;
- Look beyond the numbers. *Why* are they telling you what they are telling you?
- Measure your favors: empower yourself/stop surrendering your power to others;
- Monitor communication effectiveness – at work and at home. Insist upon high return on investment for communication efforts. Without effective and meaningful communication you are doomed to mediocrity and at the mercy of chance;

---

[198] If for no other reason than to avoid falling victim to it in the hands of others.

- Constantly Reassess Action to ensure it suits the Context in which you are standing;
- Focus on sustaining a solution-oriented mindset and not a problem-oriented one;
- Seek short-term solutions but *always* with long-term focus.

Head Space

Finally, take a little time for yourself every day. I'm not talking about sitting out on the front lawn chanting or adopting new gods from another culture. Every morning, no matter whether there's a calm at work or a storm, I daydream while I drink my coffee. I do nothing else – just sip and stare into space. I don't care what anyone says or how much they jump up and down. By now they all know there's an invisible bubble around me until I put the mug down and tune back into the world.

I also refuse to put sprinklers on the lawn. In the evenings I water the lawn manually with a garden hose. Sometimes I water in straight lines, sometimes in squares. But again, I'm daydreaming, chilling out, coming down, switching off my thinking and allowing my mind to wander onto anything not work- or problem-related. Interestingly, I usually come up with solutions to problems in the shower! Could be because it's early morning and I haven't been bombarded with nonsense by then. Could be because my subconscious was working on the problem while I was asleep or thinking about other things. Could be the ions in the water reacting with the electricity in my brain. Could just be craziness. The important point, however, is that I have three ways everyday to get some head space without locking myself away in a cabin up in the hills for days on end.

What do *you* do? Do you do anything? It doesn't take a trip or lots of time and money to sneak in some valuable head space. Resolve to do at least one thing everyday that allows you to detach, come down, gather yourself and prepare to jump back into the race in better mental condition. This is the first P – Pause – in the start of the Ten P cycle. As an aside, I have a neighbor who stands at her back door every day at exactly the same time. She just stares up at the clouds. I can see her lips moving. She's either praying, rambling to herself, building herself up – whatever. But it's always about fifteen minutes before the gang of kids get home with all their bags, books and demands for dinner. Seems she too has a coping head space method. If *you* don't have one, get one: you'll feel much better for it.

Feedback

One woman in the health industry told me that she now pauses and watches fellow workers almost as if they are part of some movie playing out before her. She told me she spotted negative people on her team who she would never previously have described as negative. She was delighted that her eyes had now been opened to what was really going on with people around her and that her decisions and actions were far more satisfactory to her than previously.

An insurance manager told me that observing and reflecting led to him discovering that one of his directors was never really listening. Instead, he was preparing to counter everything the manager had just said. As a result of this discovery he told me he now plans his conversations almost like tactical or strategic events to ensure he gets his key message through before the director's internal dialogue kicks in.

Finally, an evening student from the world of engineering told me she had quit her job. The lessons surrounding life plan, sticking with the same job while blaming others, etc, struck home for her so she left to join another company. She thanked me one evening expressing delight with her decision and relief at having found the courage to walk away. Good for her. Far too many of us ignore such advice because it usually comes from people rolling in money – easy for them to say they'd walk away if they felt they were going nowhere. But when ordinary people get out to save their own sanity and demonstrate a willingness to consider the other aspects too – self, family, health – and not just money and career, then hopefully others will learn from their example too.[199]

Some Final Thoughts

This book should lead to you talking less and listening more. It should see you always striving to know the big picture, striving to know the context in which you are standing and adapting your behavior and plans to suit. It should see you becoming more consistent – Positive Consistency – thereby moving you toward effective management of everyday things and higher order things ("leadership" according to many people). You must strive to Constantly Reassess *especially* during times of pressure, crisis, and emergency.

It must be abundantly clear to you by now that this book was about you managing you, not you managing others: we will move to that step in The 'PEOPLE' Factor: *Leading & Managing the People Around You*. For now, don't become discouraged at how it takes a long time to kill off old habits; it is incredibly difficult to maintain the discipline required to instill new ones, but the result is well worth the effort.

Don't forget to focus on the positives too. Remember, always watching out for mistakes and negatives can lead to big problems. Later, in book two, we will see how spotting the 'Successful

---

[199] As this lady demonstrated, you don't just decide you've had enough and quit your job. She planned her exit. She educated herself. She found another job. She put her finances in order.

Deviants' – the people unusually successful when compared to their peers – is a key skill when seeking to lead and manage the people around you.

From here on out, no matter what confronts you, remember, **Just Manage It!** Pause, think, break it down into chunks, use the negative feedback and reasons you are hearing to plot your way around the problem; plug into your personal and professional networks and leverage the knowledge and expertise of the people around you (more on this in book two of this series). Swap despair for management, a problem-oriented mindset for a solution oriented one, and get the job done.

Bibliography

Adair, J. (1983). *Effective Leadership.* Pan Books Ltd.: London.

Armstrong, M. (2004) *How To Be An Even Better Manager – A Complete A – Z of Proven Techniques & Essential Skills.* Sixth Edition. Kogan Page.

Aronson, E., Wilson, T. D. Akert, Robin M. (2004). *Social Psychology.* (4th ed). Pearson Education Inc. New Jersey.

Aurelius, M. (1909 – first published, 2003). *Meditations.* The Barnes & Noble Library of Essential Reading. New York.

Babcock, L. and Laschever, S. (2003). *Women Don't Ask – Negotiation And The Gender Divide.* Princeton University Press.

Belbin, R. Meredith. (2004). *Management Teams – Why They Succeed or Fail.* (2nd ed).

Belgacom: Journal of General Management. Vol 27 No. 1 (Autumn 2001).

Carayol, R. and Firth, D. (2001). *Corporate Voodoo – Principles For Business Mavericks And Magicians.* Capstone Publishing Ltd.

Carr, A. (2004) *Positive Pyschology: The Science of Happiness and Human Strengths.* Routledge: UK.

Cole, G.A. (2004). *Management Theory and Practice*. 6th Edition. Thomson.

Cynkar, A: *Whole Workplace Health*. Monitor on Psychology, March 2007 Vol. 38 No. 3.

Dalai Lama. (2002). *How to Practice - The Way to a Meaningful Life*. Rider.

Davenport, T. H., and Prusak, L. (1998, 2000). *Working Knowledge – How Organizations Manage What They Know*. Harvard Business School Press.

Dessler, G. (2004). *Management – Principles and Practices for Tomorrow's Leaders*. 3rd Edition. Pearson Education Inc.

Dennis F. (2006). *How to Get Rich – The Distilled Wisdom of One of Britain's Wealthiest Self-Made Entrepreneurs*. Ebury Press.

Descartes, R. (1637 – original, 2004). *Discourse on Method and Meditations on the First Philosophy*. Barnes & Noble Library of Essential Reading. New York.

Dyer, W. W. (1976). *Your Erroneous Zones – Escape Negative Thinking And Take Control Of Your Life*. Time Warner Books.

Edwards, P. & S., Douglas, L. C. (1998). *Getting Business To come To You – A Complete Do-It-Yourself Guide to Attracting All the Business You Can Enjoy*. 2nd Edition. Tarcher Penguin.

Fisher, R. and Ury, W. (1981, 1991). *Getting To Yes – Negotiating An Agreement Without Giving In*. Random House Business Books.

Glasser, W. (1998). *Choice Theory: A New Psychology of Personal Freedom*. HarperCollins Publishers, Inc. New York.

Goldstein, N. J., Martin, S. J., Cialdini, R. B. (2007). *Yes! – 50 Secrets From the Science of Persuasion*. Profile Books Limited.

Goleman, D. (2004) *Emotional Intelligence & Working with Emotional Intelligence*. Bloomsbury Publishing PLC.

Greenberger, D. and Padesky, C. Mind. (1995). *Over Mood: Change How You Feel by Changing the Way You Think*. The Guilford Press.

Gunnigle, P., Heraty, N. and Morley, M. J. (1997, 2002). *Human Resource Management in Ireland*. Second Edition. Gill & Macmillan.

Hall, Michael L:
www.neurosemantics.com/stuttering/egostrength.htm

Hawton, K., Salkovskis, P., Kirk, J., Clark, D. (2006). *Cognitive Behavior Therapy for Psychiatric Problems: A Practical Guide*. Oxford: Oxford University Press.

Hergenhahn, B.R., Olson, M.H. (2003). *An Introduction to Theories of Personality* (Sixth Edition). Pearson Education Inc. New Jersey.
Hofstede, G., et al (1990), *Measuring Organizational Cultures: A qualitative and Quantitative Study across Twenty cases*, in Administrative Science Quarterly 35/2.

Humphreys, T. (2006). *The Mature Manager – Managing From Inside Out*. Newleaf.

Jennings, J. (2002). *Less Is More – How Great Companies Use Productivity as a Competitive Tool in Business*. Portfolio.

Kaplan, R. S., Norton, D. P. (2001). *The Strategy-focused Organization – How Balanced Scorecard Companies Thrive in the New Business Environment.* Harvard Business School Publishing Corporation.

Kingston, W. (2003). *Innovation: The Creative Impulse in Human Progress.* The Leonard R. Sugerman Press Inc. Washington D.C.

Krames, J. A. (2005). *Jack Welch and the 4E's of Leadership – How to put GE's Leadership Formula to work in your Organization.* McGraw-Hill

Locke, J. (1690). *An Essay Concerning Human Understanding.*

Lysons, K. *Organizational Analysis.* Supplement to the British Journal of Administrative Management, No. 18, March/April 1997.

Mackay, C. (1841, 1852, 2004). *Extraordinary Popular Delusions and the Madness of Crowds.* Barnes & Noble. New York.

Manzoni, J. F., Barsoux, J. L. (2002). *The Set-Up-To-Fail Syndrome – How Good Managers Cause Great People To Fail.* Harvard Business School Publishing Corporation.

Maxwell, J. C. (2004). *Winning with People – Discover the People Principles That Work for you Every Time.* Thomas Nelson Inc.

McCormack, M. H. (1984). *What They Don't Teach You At Harvard Business School.* HarperCollins Business.

Mintzberg, H. (2004). *Manager Not MBAs – A Hard Look at the Soft Practice of Managing and Management Development.* Pearson Education Limited.

Mullins, L. J. (2005). *Management And Organizational Behavior*. 7th Edition. Pearson Education Limited.

Myers, D. (2008). *Exploriing Psychology in Modules*. (7th Edition). Worth Publishers. New York.

Okawa, R. (2002). *The Essence of Buddha – The Path to Enlightenment*. Time Warner Paperbacks.

Ormerod, P. (2005). *Why Most Things Fail – And How To Avoid It*. Faber and Faber Limited.

Pierce, V. (2003). *Quick Thinking On Your Feet*. Mercier Press. Ireland.

Peters, P. J, Waterman, R. H. (2004, 1982). *In Search of Excellence: Lessons from America's Best-Run Companies*. HarperCollins Publishers, Inc. New York.

Ranganatham, C., Watson-Manheim, M.B., Keeler, J: *Bringing Professionals On Board: Lessons on Executing IT-Enabled Organizational Transformation*. MIS quarterly Executive Vol. 3 No. 3/September 2004. (Referred to as Gemini Project in this book).

Rath, T. and Clifton, D. O. (2004). *How Full Is Your Bucket? Positive Strategies For Work and Life*. The Gallup Press.

Roberto, M. A. (2005). *Why Great Leaders Don't Take Yes for an Answer: Managing for Conflict and Consensus*. Pearson Education, Inc. New Jersey.

Robinson, G. (2004). *I'll Show Them Who's Boss – The Six Secrets Of Successful Management*. BBC Books.

Rosenthal, Robert: *Covert Communication in Laboratories, Classrooms, and the Truly Real World*. Current Directions in Psychological Science, 12, 2003, 151-154.

Rotter, J. B. *Generalized expectancies for internal versus external control of reinforcement*. Psychological Monographs, 1966

Scaturo, D. J. (2005). *Clinical Dilemmas in Psychotherapy: A Transtheoretical Approach to Psychotherapy Integration*. American Psychological Association.

Schiffman, S. (2007). *Cold Calling Techniques: That Really Work*. Adams Media: Massachusetts.

Scholtes, S. *Ratings game that turned into a guessing game*. Financial Times Sept 29/Sept 30 2007.
Stanton, N. (2004). *Mastering Communication*. 4th Edition. Palgrave Macmillan.

Sutton, R. (2007). *The No Asshole Rule – Building a Civilized Workplace and Surviving One That Isn't*. Sphere.

Sternberg, R. (1997). *Successful Intelligence*. New York. Plume.

Templar, R. (2005). *The Rules of Management*. Pearson Prentice Hall Business.

Templar, R. (2006). *The Rules of Life*. Pearson Prentice Hall.

Tesser, A. and Phalus, D. (1983): *The definition of Self: private and public self evaluation management strategies*. Journal of Personality and Social Psychology 44: 672-82.

Thompson, M. (1995, 2000, 2003). *Teach Yourself Philosophy*. Hodder & Stoughton Limited.

Toffler, A. (1980). *The Third Wave*. Bantam Books. United States.

Tracy B. (1993). *Maximum Achievement – Strategies and Skills That Will Unlock Your Hidden Powers to Succeed*. Simon and Schuster Paperbacks.

Trump, D. J. (1997). *Trump: The Art of the Comeback*. Crown Business.

Tzu, Sun. (1981). *The Art of War*. Hodder Mobius.

Vecchio, R. P. (2006). *Organizational Behavior – Core Concepts*. International Student Edition. 6th Edition. Thomson South-Western.

Watkins, M. (2003). *The First 90 Days: Critical Success Strategies for New Leaders at all Levels*. Harvard Business School Publishing. Massachusetts.

Wiersema & Bantel (1991). See Journal of General Management 2001.

Wilde, G. (2001). *Target Risk 2: A New Psychology of Health and Safety: What Works, What Doesn't and Why…* Toronto: PDE Publications.

Wilson, T. & Fairburn, C. (1998). *Mediation of change in CBT for bulimia nervosa*. Paper presented at the Mechanisms of Change in Cognitive Behavior Therapy Conference, Center for Advanced Study in the Behavioral Sciences, Stanford, CT.

Yukl, G. (2006). *Leadership In Organizations*. 6th Edition. Pearson Prentice Hall.

The Second Book in the **Just Mange It!** series:

The 'PEOPLE' Factor:
Leading and Managing the People Around You

You have learned to manage yourself, to get out of your own way, to avoid adding to your own difficulties. You have learned to observe those around you, to see what is really going on. Now it's time to start managing the people around you more effectively. The 'PEOPLE' Factor is the second book in the **Just Manage It!** series. Building upon the foundations of the first book – *If You Cannot Manage YOURSELF You Cannot Manage Others* – the second in the series touches upon everyday concerns of managers around the world:

Bureaucracy	Employee Development
Motivation	Organizational Culture
Managing Change	Micro-Management
Communication	Managing Delegation
Training	Managing Presenteeism

Some of the concepts discussed in the second book include:

- The Five-Rs of Delegation
- Healthy Troublemakers
- The Propensity Factor
- The Five most powerful words in management
- The danger of personnel files
- Resident Rebels
- Negative synergies
- Presenteeism and employee engagement problems
- Effective Listening

Go to www.JustManageIt.com for further details.

www.ingramcontent.com/pod-product-compliance
Lightning Source LLC
Chambersburg PA
CBHW051802170526
45167CB00005B/1842